ISRAEL, THE MIDDLE EAST, AND U.S. INTERESTS

ISRAEL, THE MIDDLE EAST, AND U.S. INTERESTS

edited by
Harry S. Allen
Ivan Volgyes

introduction by
Edmund S. Muskie

PRAEGER

PRAEGER SPECIAL STUDIES • PRAEGER SCIENTIFIC

Library of Congress Cataloging in Publication Data

Main entry under title:

Israel, the Middle East, and U.S. interests.

  Bibliography: p.
  Includes index.
  1. Near East—Politics and government—1945—
—Addresses, essays, lectures. I. Allen, Harry S.,
1923–   II. Völgyes, Ivan, 1936–
DS63.1.I78 1983   956'.04   82-22357
ISBN 0-03-063431-8

Published in 1983 by Praeger Publishers
CBS Educational and Professional Publishing
a Division of CBS Inc.
521 Fifth Avenue, New York, New York 10175 U.S.A.

© 1983 by Praeger Publishers

All rights reserved

3456789   052   987654321

Printed in the United States of America

CONTENTS

	Page
PREFACE	vii
ACKNOWLEDGMENTS	xi
INTRODUCTION by Edmund S. Muskie	xiii

Chapter

PART I

BETWEEN WAR AND PEACE: CONFLICT IN THE MIDDLE EAST

1 JEWS, JUDAISM, AND THE LAND OF ISRAEL: A HISTORICAL PERSPECTIVE
   Todd M. Endelman 3

2 REQUIREMENTS FOR A STABLE PEACE: ARAB AND ISRAELI IMAGES
   Abdul Aziz Said and Alain Sportiche 18

3 CHANGE IN THE MIDDLE EAST: IS THERE A CHANCE FOR PEACE?
   Haim Shaked 26

PART II

WE OFFER A CHANCE FOR GROWTH: ISRAELI AGRICULTURE AS A GROWTH MODEL FOR THE REGION

4 ISRAELI RANGELANDS AND THE MIDDLE EAST
   Cyrus M. McKell 37

5 THE IRRIGATION PROBLEM: THE ISRAELI EXPERIENCE
   C. Don Gustafson 51

Chapter		Page

PART III

THE UNITED STATES AND THE MIDDLE EAST

6   THE PARAMETERS OF U.S. POLICY IN THE PERSIAN GULF AND THE MIDDLE EAST
Amos Perlmutter   67

7   U.S. POLICY IN IRAN AND THE ISLAMIC REVIVAL FOR THE MIDDLE EAST
Nikki R. Keddie   73

8   ISRAEL'S CONTRIBUTION TO U.S. INTERESTS IN THE MIDDLE EAST
Michael Handel   80

PART IV

THE SOVIET UNION AND THE MIDDLE EAST

9   SOVIET INTERESTS IN THE MIDDLE EAST
Alvin Z. Rubinstein   89

10   FAITHFUL AGENTS AND HONEST BROKERS: EASTERN EUROPEAN POLICIES IN THE MIDDLE EAST
Trond Gilberg   105

11   SOVIET POLICY IN THE MIDDLE EAST: IN SEARCH OF ANALYTICAL FRAMEWORKS
Vernon V. Aspaturian   126

PART V

CONCLUSION

12   THE AUTONOMY TALKS: MIDDLING THROUGH
James Leonard   153

INDEX   165

ABOUT THE EDITORS AND CONTRIBUTORS   169

PREFACE

Few regions of the world have possessed a more volatile history than that which has been dubbed the Arc of Crisis. Extending roughly from Iran to the northern and southern edges of the Mediterranean and from Turkey to perhaps Morocco, this area has been the cradle of civilization and the repository of culture as much as the grave of empires and the battleground of nations, cultures, and religions throughout the last six thousand years of recorded history.

It has been, of course, not one unified region but a mosaic in which states and empires alternated with great alacrity, fortunes of people and races changed over short or long historical periods, and passions fanned by a constant and unabating sun ran as red hot as the source of our solar power itself. Solomon's armies conquered here and Darius swept across the region; Alexander the Great died where the Romans beat down their enemies; the flags of Islam and of Israel were raised here and crusaders and Turks put the torch to those who dared doubt their convictions and power; Napoleon marched and Britons paraded their might here; and U.S. marines descended on Tripoli and Soviet technicians prepared Arab aircraft to strike into Israel. The flames of the oil fields threw light on the power potential of the region, while board rooms, prices, and nations trembled as the newfound power was exercised; the Soviets stared bemusedly as chanting masses demanded death to 52 U.S. diplomats in the ancient capital of Tehran, where a mere few years ago the United States shared in the three thousandth anniversary celebration of the Persian Empire; and stargazing fanatics prepared to assassinate one of the greatest peacemakers of the region, President Anwar Sadat of Egypt. Such is the legacy of the region with which this volume is concerned.

This book, of course, is not a history or a summary accounting of the region of the Middle East. The editors and the authors did not try to address every issue, every confrontation that has marred the peace of the region. After all, such a simple task as merely accounting for the 40-odd conflicts of the Middle East that have erupted among the various Arab states since their establishment after World War II—not to mention the conflicts between the state of Israel and its neighbors—would fill the pages of many laborious volumes. On the contrary, this book attempts to focus on those dimensions of the region that possibly can affect the safety and security of the United States in its relations with the Middle East generally and with Israel specifically.

In our selection of the articles for this volume, we have tried to offer some common themes that tie the peace process together, which could provide a perspective on the process that began with the arrival of President Anwar Sadat in Tel Aviv, the act that opened the door, however haltingly and slowly, to peace in the region. We concentrated on the requirements of peace, bringing together those voices that share the hope that such peace is indeed possible and, if a reality, can be based on common values of tranquility, justice, and progress for all. Having thus set our task, for Part I of this volume we searched for insights into those areas of research necessary for a comprehension of the complexity of the problem, ranging from the real difficulties of coexistence to the perceptual distinctions that make it impossible for the region's peoples to understand each other's position regarding the present—and the future—of the land where they must live side by side.

A special point, not dealt with elsewhere, has been singled out in this volume, a circumstance that offers concrete hope for the future cooperation of the various peoples and states in the region: this is the contribution Israel has made—and is capable of making ever more greatly in the future—to agrarian development. Making the desert bloom has long been the goal of the settlers of Israel, and this agricultural miracle offers special potential for all the area's people in attempting to supply ever-growing populations with enough food. If there are areas of future cooperation, they may begin in the exchange of varied experiences in attaining agricultural growth—people learning not the art of making war but, rather, the craft of growing tomatoes for all the children to share.

Sadly but perhaps most important, this volume must address the problems of world politics and the interests of the great powers in the region. For the two superpowers, the United States and the USSR, the Middle East has offered ample opportunity for the extension of power. For the United States, the region has become a vital strategic concern: in hostile hands it could deprive us of oil; reduce our geopolitical room to maneuver; and deprive us of our ability to help our oldest ally in the region, the state of Israel. The Soviet Union has an enormous stake in the region as well. Aside from negatively impacting on the United States, a Soviet presence in the region could lead to Soviet control of the Mediterranean and the Persian Gulf as well as the waterways of the richest oil-producing nations of the world.

The chapters in the main body of this book tie together many of the major problems and conflicts of the Arc of Crisis. The authors, all of them specialists with impressive professional and personal contributions to the scholarship concerning the region, originally composed their studies for the Israel, the Middle East, and U.S. National

Interests symposium held at the University of Nebraska in Lincoln, April 8-10, 1981. They were joined by two individuals whose commitment to peace in the Middle East is as impressive as the keynote addresses they delivered and the chapters they provided for this volune. The Honorable Edmund S. Muskie, former secretary of state under whose auspices the Camp David peace treaty largely developed, and Ambassador James Leonard, deputy special negotiator for the Middle East during the Carter administration, in their introductory and closing articles, respectively, both deal with the difficult process of attaining peace in the Middle East. Their ideals and suggestions, their goals and aspirations for the people of the region are offered here to provide a glimpse of the possibilities for peace in this troubled part of the world, a vision that we the editors, who were also the organizers of this conference, fervently share.

ACKNOWLEDGMENTS

The symposium at which these studies were presented was funded by grants from the Nebraska Committee for the Humanities, a state program of the National Endowment for the Humanities, the University of Nebraska Foundation, and the Cooper Foundation. Additional support was provided by the University of Nebraska Office of the President and the following University of Nebraska-Lincoln (UNL) components: Office of the Chancellor, Institute of Agriculture and Natural Resources, College of Arts and Sciences, and the University Program Council. In addition, the following corporate donors were generous in their support of the symposium: Internorth, United States National Bank, Omaha National Bank, Northwestern Bell Telephone Company, Valmont Industries, Coopers and Lybrand, American National Bank, Mutual of Omaha/United of Omaha, First National Bank of Lincoln, the Lincoln office of E. F. Hutton, National Bank of Commerce-Lincoln, and Commonwealth Electric.

The following persons and groups provided help in various aspects of the original symposium: Nebraska Educational Television Consortium for Higher Education; the Nebraska Art Association; Norman Geske, Director, Sheldon Gallery; Omaha-Council Bluffs Region of the National Conference of Christians and Jews; Dean Max Larsen, College of Arts and Sciences; Dr. Ronald Roskens, President, University of Nebraska; Dr. Robert Rutford, Interim Chancellor, UNL; Dr. Martin Massengale, Vice-chancellor, Institute of Agriculture and Natural Resources, UNL; Mr. Robert Mussman, Director of Public Information, UNL; Anti-Defamation League of B'nai B'rith, Plains States Region; Mr. Ron Bowlin, Director, Kimball Recital Hall; Dr. Ronald W. Wright, Vice-chancellor, Business and Finance, UNL; and Dr. Gerald Rudolph, Dean of Libraries, UNL.

INTRODUCTION
Edmund S. Muskie

In every administration there is an effort on the part of its public relations elements to coin historic phrases: some of them live, some of them do not. To the extent that those phrases or slogans are substitutes for substance, they are not particularly helpful. In the Carter administration, there was one phrase that has survived and will probably live on, coined by Zbigniew Brzezinski: the Arc of Crisis. He used it to describe the geographical sweep stretching from the Eastern Mediterranean to Southwest Asia, and surely he was right. Today, no region of the world holds more importance or more danger for the rest of the globe.

What we are likely to forget, so obsessed are we with our own time and emergencies, is that this region was a cockpit of crisis long before the state of Israel was established in 1948 and long before the industrial democracies developed their present thirst for oil.

The most ancient scripts, as well as today's headlines, tell us that the region is a mosaic of many peoples, diverse religions, and competing ethnic loyalties. Indeed, some struggles in the region, such as the struggle between Arabs and Persians or the struggle of the Israeli people to find secure existence, predate the dawn of modern Western civilization.

Knowing this should invest us with persistence and patience; we can hardly hope for instant solutions to problems whose roots are in antiquity. What makes these ancient problems infinitely more volatile is the atmosphere of rapid and destructive change, not to mention the intense interests of outsiders. This region, this Arc of Crisis, holds many of the world's richest resources and many of its poorest people. It is the home to ancient cultures and traditions, which are colliding with the pressures of modernization. It is the focus of great power rivalries. The result of all of this is instability and turmoil.

I can remember the days when the phrase "the Middle East crisis" brought to mind the confrontation between Israel and its Arab neighbors. In recent years, that phrase has come to encompass multiple crises. Let me list only a few to illustrate my point.

In the Persian Gulf end of the Arc the Soviet Union has invaded and attempted to subjugate Afghanistan—an event of potentially ominous significance not only for that land, but for the industrial democracies that move roughly one-fifth of their oil through the Persian Gulf. Iran, once considered a friend and military bulwark for the West after Britain reduced its presence east of the Suez, is now in the grip of domestic revolution, war with Iraq, and economic crisis, and it is rapidly being wooed by the Soviet Union to cast its loyalties with a regime Ayatollah Khomeini once described as an atheistic demon. Turkey is ravaged by debt, inflation, and domestic political turmoil. Lebanon has in recent years been caught up in a web of violence and civil war. Hostilities along the border between North and South Yemen have threatened the stability of the Arabian peninsula and have raised the potential for mischief by the Soviet client in a vital spot. The restlessness of Palestinian Arabs has given rise to terrorist activities that not only affect the immediate area but also break out elsewhere across the globe. Finally, although peace has been established between Israel and Egypt and the framework laid for a final settlement, the task of building a comprehensive peace between Israel and its neighbors remains unfinished.

This is quite a litany. It is almost an invitation to discouragement, if not despair. Reciting it brings to mind a story told by Carl Sandburg in his poem "The People, Yes." In the story a policeman comes upon a would-be suicide preparing to jump from a bridge. "Hold it, man," he says, and hoping to prevent a tragedy, the policeman kindly invites the wretched man to talk about his troubles. In the end, however, after hearing the man's sad tale, the policeman decides to jump, too.

Of course, it is not my purpose here to suggest we jump, too—that we open ourselves to despair. We must never conclude that because it is beyond our power to <u>control</u> events in this troubled region, we should not try to <u>influence</u> them. I want to suggest that we steer a course between euphoria and despair, that we seek to identify clearly our own interests, that we ask what we can do—we, the Western industrial nations whose interests in the region are both economic and spiritual.

It would be both arrogant and futile to suggest that we can solve quickly or decisively the multiple problems of the region. But we of the West are powerful and influential, and we do have legitimate interests to protect, the least of which are our own peace and survival. What then can we do?

The beginning of wisdom, it seems to me, is to come to a clear understanding of what our vital interests are. We are the industrialized democracies—the United States, Canada, Western Europe, and Japan. We have a vital interest in seeing local disputes confined and settled. It is a sad commentary on modern history that local wars often widen into broader conflict. Facing the local tangle of conflict in the Middle East, our best course is to work tirelessly and collectively for peace.

The Camp David process is an example of how we should proceed and a warning of how vulnerable and filled with frustration even the most successful efforts can be. But however great the obstacles to peace are, we have no choice but to seek it. As President Eisenhower said years ago in another context, "There is today no alternative to peace; there's also no alternative to peacemaking and we must persist in it."

Second, we have a vital interest in protecting the independence and autonomy of all states in the region. Precisely because it is a region of crisis, the Middle East is vulnerable to mischief by outside powers. The same characteristics that make the region a challenge to peacemakers make it a magnet for troublemakers. While I think it is dangerous to hold the Soviet Union responsible for every unhappy event in the region, it is clear that the Soviets have a history of ambition in the Middle East. The Soviet effort to crush Afghanistan adds an ominous unfinished paragraph to that history. We of the West can live with free autonomous states in the Middle East, even when we have our differences with them; what we cannot accept is domination of that region by any outside power.

Third, we have a vital interest in sound, correct, mutually beneficial relations with the peoples of the Arab world. The ability of the industrial democracies to define their vital interests in the region will depend on our relationship with the Arab states. We have an abiding interest in assuring that the balance of power and influence in the region does not turn against the West. And, if the West hopes to play a creative role in fostering a settlement between Israel and the Arab world, it is important that we are able to discuss the aspects of a common peace in an atmosphere of common purpose rather than one of hostility. In recent years, of course, the energy issue has made the West more sensitive in its relations with the Arab countries. But even if that issue could be resolved overnight—though it cannot—correct constructive relations would still be important to us, to them, and to world peace.

Finally, and perhaps most important, the West has a vital interest in the security, the strength, and the well-being of the state of Israel. About this matter I have feelings that are deeply personal as well as hardheadedly practical.

A commitment to Israel has been part of my public life for 35 years. I visited Israel and flew over Masada in a helicopter provided by Golda Meir. I have visited the underground shelters used to protect the children of Israel along the Golan Heights border, and I have visited the Golan Heights and observed firsthand the vulnerability of those who live below. I have had the opportunity and privilege of discussing these issues with the leaders of Israel and Egypt.

But I am moved by more than personal emotion or respect for the spiritual kinship between Israel and its supporters in the West. There are soberly practical reasons to stand by Israel. Even in the age when the United States is feeling a "strategic consensus" for the region, Israel is a strategic asset for the West. It is a living example of democracy at work in the Middle East and a showcase of the modernization-and-development idea, an idea that could well serve other nations in the area. Israel has shown that modern development can take place in harmony with ancient values and traditions.

Israel is, moreover, a test of Western constancy and devotion to its commitments. The West will gain nothing in the long run—not respect or energy advantages or lasting peace—by wavering in its support for Israel. The Arab world understands that we will not allow ourselves to be sinisterly pulled away from our old friends. We will not buy friendship or oil at the expense of Israel. Indeed, I am convinced that it is by making this pact clear that we can command respect of all the nations of the Middle East and contribute to peace in the region. And it is illuminative that all nations in that region still talk to the United States as a possible influence serving each of their interests.

These are the vital interests we must protect: peace in the area; the independence of states in the region; good relations with all peoples; and security, safety, and peace for Israel. How can we promote these interests? What policies should we pursue? In addition to the policies that are implied by the interests I have described, I would suggest others.

We must be strong. I do not believe that military power is sufficient to keep the peace, but I do believe it is necessary. Ironically, President Reagan and his administration will be the beneficiaries of efforts in this regard launched by his predecessor, notably, the rapid deployment force. If we are to protect our friends and make creditable our pledges to defend our interests, we must be ready to maintain our strength and to strengthen our friends.

We must pursue energy independence. This policy is, of course, related to the first, for dependent nations are not strong. The longer the West remains vulnerable to interruptions in its energy supplies, the longer the danger will persist that the policies of one of us or some of us can be bought or taken hostage. That is unacceptable, and it is an argument for the most intense efforts to free the industrial democracies from energy dependence on the Middle East or from any potentially hostile force. Above all, we must stand together and stand by our friends. The interests of the West will be served by the unity of the West. Those interests, as I have said, will be served also by fidelity to allies like Israel.

Have we any cause for optimism? At the beginning of my remarks I listed several sources of uncertainty and turmoil in the Middle East. The region fully reflects Whitehead's phrase: "It is the business of the future to be dangerous."

But these are also times of opportunity in the region. That is true in major part because of the courage of three national leaders—President Carter, the late President Sadat, and Prime Minister Begin—and the hopeful new reality they have created. Our task for the future is clear: We must resist impatience, and we must not give way to the lure of simple answers, to those who think slogans are solutions. We must recognize our interests and be prepared to defend them. If we do, we help define the fate of the Middle East, our role there, and the well-being of much of the world for the rest of this century and beyond.

We cannot predict the future, but we can help shape it. As G. K. Chesterton once put it, "I do not believe in a fate that strikes man no matter how they act, but I do believe in a fate that strikes man unless they act."

PART I

BETWEEN WAR AND PEACE:
CONFLICT IN THE MIDDLE EAST

1

JEWS, JUDAISM, AND THE LAND OF ISRAEL: A HISTORICAL PERSPECTIVE

TODD M. ENDELMAN

Western observers of the contemporary Middle East frequently remark that the "Land of Israel" is a holy land for three faiths[1]— Judaism, Christianity, and Islam. While not incorrect, this observation requires amplification because it obscures the nature of each religion's relationship to the Land and implies that it is equally sacred for all three faiths in precisely the same way. In fact, there is a profound asymmetry to Jewish, Christian, and Islamic links to the Land of Israel.[2] The relationship of Jews to the Land has been qualitatively different than that of adherents of the other two faiths. In part, this can be traced to the early history of the Jewish people in the Land of Israel, the nature of their faith as it developed there, and, in part, to the dual character of Jewish group identity throughout history, being simultaneously religious and national.

For Christianity, the Land of Israel has been first and foremost the Holy Land of Jesus and his disciples. The sacred character of the Land for Christians has derived from its being the scene of the earthly life of Jesus. Although Christianity accepted the sacred scriptures of the Jews, seeing itself as the spiritual descendant of the biological Israel, it never took much interest in the pre-Christian sites of Israelite history. Rather, it treasured those places associated by tradition with the birth, career, and death of Jesus and, to a lesser extent, his closest followers. From the time of Constantine, these sites, on which churches and monasteries were erected, attracted pilgrims and penitents from all corners of the Christian world. Theo-

---

I wish to thank my colleague Lawrence Fine for the many helpful suggestions and references that he gave me while I was preparing this chapter.

logically, however, the Land of Israel played no decisive role in Christian thinking about salvation (although some millenarians placed the early stages of the Second Coming in Jerusalem),[3] nor did its soil possess any intrinsically sacred quality aside from the specific holy places in Jerusalem, Bethlehem, and the Galilee. Institutionally as well, it counted for little in the hierarchical, bureaucratic life of the church. For the West, Rome was the center of the Christian universe (at least until the Reformation), not Jerusalem.

For Islam, the Land of Israel in its entirety has never been regarded as sacred territory. Rather, Islamic interest has focused on Jerusalem and, in particular, on the Temple mount with its twin shrines, the Dome of the Rock, and the Aksa mosque. According to Muslim tradition, a winged horselike beast transported Muhammad from Arabia to this site in a single night, and from there Muhammad ascended to heaven, where his prophetic predecessors confirmed his mission. Early Islam incorporated Jewish and Christian notions of the holiness of Jerusalem, so that the city became the third central sanctuary of Islam, after Mecca and Medina. Some Muslim traditions, which were not universally accepted, taught that Jerusalem would be the scene of the Resurrection and the Last Judgment. In this century, the conflict between Arab and Jewish nationalism has intensified Muslim veneration for Jerusalem to the extent that Jerusalem has assumed an importance in Islamic thinking that it never enjoyed previously. Historically, however, the Land of Israel played a relatively insignificant role in the development of Islam. There is no evidence that Muhammad ever set foot in the Land—after all, the Arabian peninsula was the birthplace of Islam, not the Land of Israel—and Arab armies did not conquer the Land until several years after Muhammad's death. Most of the shrines outside Jerusalem that Muslims venerate (for example, the tomb of the patriarchs in Hebron) are of Jewish or Christian origin and were appropriated by the Arabs after their occupation of the Land, in some cases many centuries later. Politically Jerusalem was never an important Muslim capital, while intellectually it was never a preeminent center of scholarship.

The historical links of Jews and Judaism to the Land of Israel have been of an entirely different character. Both Judaism as a religion and the Jews as a nation originated in the Land. The earliest history of the Jewish people, from the origins of the tribal confederacy in the twelfth century B.C.E. (before the common era) until the Babylonian exile in the sixth century B.C.E., unfolded there, and the record of that history became the sacred scripture of Judaism—the Hebrew Bible. The religious faith of Jews in later centuries was inseparable from their understanding of these earliest chapters in their history. They believed that at the dawn of history God had made a covenant with the patriarchs, in which he had promised them and their descendants the Land of Israel as a perpetual inheritance, and that later he had renewed his promise to David and Solomon and their successors.[4] When Jews in antiquity or in the medieval world read a biblical passage such as the following, they understood it in a literal manner as historical fact:

> And the Lord said to Abram, after Lot had parted from him, "Raise your eyes and look out from where you are, to the north and south, to the east and west, for I give all the land that you see to you and your offspring forever. I will make your offspring as the dust of the earth, so that if one can count the dust of the earth, then your offspring too can be counted. Up, walk about the land, through its length and its breadth, for I give it to you."[5]

In short, the Land of Israel was the Promised Land.

The loss of independence, the destruction of the Temple, and the exile of the Judean elite in the early sixth century B.C.E. challenged the covenantal idea, as did the abortive revolt against Rome in the years 66-70 C.E., which culminated in the destruction of Jerusalem. In both instances, history posed the same questions: Why had Jewish sovereignty over the Land come to an end and Why were the Jewish people (or at least some of them) in exile? The answers of the postexilic prophets, in the first instance, and of the rabbis, in the second, were similar: an omnipotent God, who guided the fate of the Jewish people, had punished them for disregarding his commandments, which they had sworn to observe. Having ignored its covenantal obligations, Israel had been exiled from its land. However, both prophets and rabbis stressed that the Exile would not last forever but was, rather, a temporary condition. The natural place of the Jewish people was in the Land of Israel. For the rabbis, the Romans were interlopers, their rule illegitimate. The divine promise would be fulfilled in its entirety some day and the Jews would be restored to their only authentic home. Thus, until the modern period, Jews viewed the Land of Israel not only as the territory from which they and their faith had emerged but also as the point to which they would return in the future.

Before the rise of modern varieties of Judaism in the nineteenth century, all Jews conceived of their return to the Land in messianic terms.[6] They believed that the God of Israel, at a time of his choosing, would intervene in history to bring the Exile to a close. A divinely annointed messiah, descended from the Davidic royal house, would gather in the exiles from the far reaches of the Dispersion, reestablish Jewish sovereignty over the Land, rebuild the Temple, restore its sacrificial system, and initiate a golden age for the Jewish people. There was little doctrinal agreement on how this would work out in detail, probably because most messianic speculation occurred outside the framework of halakic (legal) discussions and, thus, had no immediate consequences for daily conduct. In the Talmud and the Midrash, the messianic age is usually portrayed in visionary terms: Jerusalem would be adorned with lush gardens and precious stones and strengthened by thousands of fortresses and towers; crops would ripen and trees would yield fruit every few weeks; and the righteous would feast at a great banquet on the flesh of the mythical creatures Leviathan, Behemoth, and Ziz. In certain apocalyptic writings of the early medieval period, there are extravagant, highly fanciful accounts of the beginnings of the messianic age. According to several texts, divine clouds would accompany the returning Jews and divine springs would sustain them on their journey to the Holy Land.[7] On the other hand, the sober twelfth-century philosopher and jurist Moses ben Maimon (1135-1204), or Maimonides, cautioned his readers not to expect the laws of nature to be set aside in the messianic age: "The world will follow its normal course." To be sure, hunger, jealously, strife, and war would disappear, goodness and delight would abound, and knowledge of the Lord would multiply. But Maimonides felt that no one could know the details of the age until it occurred and insisted that "a man must never ponder over legendary accounts, nor dwell upon interpretations dealing with them or with matters like them."[8] Yet despite differences such as these about the unfolding of the messianic age, there was a consensus on the fundamental point that the Jewish people would enjoy a messianic future in the Land of Israel.

It must be stressed that the belief in the ingathering of the exiles and the restoration of Jewish sovereignty was not an abstract theological doctrine. Rather, it was a vital and integral part of Jewish consciousness in the premodern world. Ritual and liturgy were suffused with references to the rebuilding of Jerusalem.[9] In the grace recited after every meal in which bread was eaten, Jews prayed: "Speedily rebuild Jerusalem the holy city in our days. Blessed are You, Lord, who in mercy will rebuild Jerusalem." And three times every day (except on Sabbaths and Festivals), Jews petitioned God to restore the glory of Jerusalem: "Return in mercy to Jerusalem Your city and dwell within it as You have spoken. Rebuild it soon within our days, as an everlasting building. Speedily set up the throne of David within it. Blessed are You, Lord, who will rebuild Jerusalem." The destruction of the Temple was not only marked by the annual observance of a day of fasting and prayer (Tisha be-Av, the ninth day of the Hebrew month of Av), when Jews read the Book of Lamentations in the synagogue, but also by the inclusion of symbolic reminders of the event in otherwise festive celebrations. In early modern Germany, for example, at the meal held in the home of the groom after the completion of the betrothal agreement, a plate would be broken as a reminder of the destruction of the Temple and the guests would take home the pieces. At feasts an empty space would be left at the table, the place not set, also as a memorial to Jerusalem's fall.[10] And in Jewish communities almost everywhere the wedding ceremony would conclude with the groom crushing a glass beneath his right foot—an act understood over the centuries (whatever its origins and latent meaning) as a sign of mourning for the loss of Jerusalem. Thus, all Jews, regardless of their theological sophistication, were continually reminded that their destiny as a people was linked to the Land of Israel.

The inclusion of prayers for the restoration of Jerusalem in the liturgy was the work of the first generations of rabbis after 70 C.E. The impulse to compose these petitions stemmed from the belief that redemption would come in the imaginable future. They did not envision the Jewish people remaining in exile for millenia nor conceive of the coming of the Messiah as an incalculably distant event. Their faith in the relative immediacy of the Return also led them to continue to study and teach laws pertaining to the Temple and its priesthood. Although these laws had ceased to have any practical importance in the daily lives of Jews after 70 C.E., the rabbis believed that they would be renewed in a not-too-distant future and, thus, could not be allowed to fall into desuetude. Such thinking led the rabbis of late-second-century Palestine to include the minutiae of priestly duties and Temple ritual and architecture in the first post-biblical collection of Jewish law, the Mishnah.[11] Once incorporated into a legal corpus believed to be of divine origin, these laws, as well as those pertaining to agricultural practices in the Land, could not be omitted or dislodged. Even after the hope of restoration had been relegated to an obscure future, the medieval rabbis of the Muslim East and the Christian West continued to work with these historically obsolete legal materials. Since the study of Jewish law (halakah) was the central intellectual activity of the premodern Jewish world, the inclusion of these topics further reenforced the centrality of the Land of Israel in Jewish religious consciousness. At the same time, the inability of pious Jews to observe Jewish law in its entirety—about one third of rabbinic law is contingent on residence in the Land itself—strengthened the feeling that Jewish life in the Diaspora was abnormal. The Torah itself remained partially unfulfilled as long as Israel was in exile. Only the Return to Zion would permit Jews to observe the Torah in all its fullness.

The importance of the Land of Israel for the rabbis of late antiquity and the middle ages was not merely halakic, however. There was as well a spiritual dimension to their longing for an end to their dispersion. For them the Land itself was hallowed. It possessed a sacred quality absent in other parts of the world. Although Jews might lead holy lives elsewhere, worshipping and serving God in the required fashion, they remained spiritually handicapped nevertheless. In the Land of Israel, the rabbis taught, religious experience took on a deeper, more intense quality. Prophecy had been bestowed only on those who had dwelled within the Land or those who had prophesied for the sake of the Land, like Daniel and Ezekiel. Prayer was more efficacious there: "When anyone prays in Jerusalem it is as if he worshipped before the Throne of Glory, for the gate of heaven is there and it is wide open for the Lord to hear."[12] Emphasis on the heightened spiritual quality of life within the Land led to the corollary belief that life in the Diaspora was spiritually incomplete. Being in exile meant not only political subjugation to Muslim and Christian overlords but spiritual deprivation as well—living in an unnatural fashion in a temporary and unfortunate condition. The quintessential expression of this feeling is to be found in a poem by the greatest of medieval Jewish poets, Yehudah Ha-Levi (circa 1075-1141).

> My heart is in the East, and I in the depths of the West.
> My food has no taste. How can it be sweet?
> How can I fulfill my pledges and my vows,
> When Zion is in the power of Edom, and I in the fetters
>   of Arabia?
> It will be nothing to me to leave all the goodness of Spain.
> So rich will it be to see the dust of the ruined sanc-
>   tuary.[13]

Yehudah Ha-Levi's longing for Zion was not merely a literary conceit. He abandoned the comforts and pleasures of the Spanish-Jewish courtier class to which he belonged by birth and in which he was widely celebrated and set out on the perilous journey to the Holy Land in 1140.[14] (Contrary to legend, it does not appear that he succeeded in reaching it.) In his mature years he had come to see Jewish life outside the Land of Israel as crippled and stunted, incomplete and deficient. Because the Land was in special favor with God, no human function could be perfect except there. Jews were less than they should be in the Diaspora. As he wrote in his religious-philosophical treatise <u>Kuzari</u>, "Sincere devotion and purity of life reach perfection only in a place which is believed to have a special relation to God."[15]

It would be misleading, however, to portray the yearning for Zion as only, or even largely, a quest for spiritual fulfillment. Though expressed frequently in an unworldly fashion, the desire for redemption was as much political as religious, for the concept of redemption in Judaism has always been national in character. The liberation of the Jewish people from the yoke of foreign oppression was inseparable from the religious vision of the ingathering of the exiles and the restoration of Jerusalem. In a particularly moving passage in his Kuzari, Yehudah Ha-Levi, who had an intimate knowledge of the political tightrope walked by Jewish courtiers in Muslim Spain, gave expression to the dual character of Jewish hopes for redemption.

> I seek freedom—from the service of those numerous people only whose favour I shall never obtain even if I work for it all my life and which would not profit me, even if I could obtain it: I mean the service of men and the courting of their favour. But I seek the service of One whose favour is obtained with the smallest effort and profits in this world and the next: this is the favour of God; His service is freedom, and humility before Him is true honour.[16]

The desire for release from political subjugation manifested itself periodically in waves of messianic agitation and excitement. The triumphant appearance of the Arabs and the Muslim caliphate on the world scene brought about an upsurge of messianism. In the mid-640s, to cite only one example, a Jew in Babylonia asserted that the messiah had come and, gathering around him some four hundred men, burned down three Christian churches and murdered the local ruler. A military force eventually captured him and his followers. He was crucified in his native village, his followers and their families slain.[17] Other great political upheavals, such as the Crusades, the Mongol advance into Europe, and the fall of Constantinople, also stimulated messianic expectations. In some cases, rumors circulated and hopes awakened, but the messiah himself never materialized; in others, charismatic figures actually assumed the messianic mantle and prepared to lead the Jews back to their own land. Frequently messianic leaders undertook military campaigns to release their people from bondage. In Kurdistan in the mid twelfth century, David Alroy assembled a substantial Jewish army and captured the Muslim fortress of Amadiyah in the mountains of Azerbaijan, with the intention of eventually fighting his way through to the Holy Land.[18] The most powerful messianic explosion in Jewish history—the movement around Shabbetai Zevi in the 1660s—swept up thousands of Jews in both the Christian and Muslim worlds.[19] In many communities families sold their possessions in expectation of an immediate return to the Land of Israel. Gluckel of Hameln (1646-1724) recalled in her famous autobiography how her father-in-law abandoned his home in Hameln, leaving things just as they were, and prepared to depart from Hamburg for the Holy Land. He sent two big barrels, containing linen, peas, smoked meat, and dried fruit, to Gluckel, who was then living in Hamburg. The barrels remained in her home for four years, her father-in-law always expecting to need them at a moment's notice for his journey.[20]

The messianic movements that punctuate Jewish history usually collapsed before their supporters sighted Zion's coastline—or came anywhere near it, for that matter. In any case, the connection between Jews and the Land did not depend on the realization of messianic hopes but on the promise of their eventual realization. At the same time, the connection to the Land was strengthened by a more tangible reality: the presence of a continuous Jewish settlement in the Holy Land from antiquity to the present.[21] For despite hardships and dangers, some Jews always remained there, even during the most disastrous periods, and occasionally they were joined by small groups of returning Jews. Substantial numbers of Jews continued to live in the Land after the destruction of Jerusalem in 70 C.E. and the Hadrianic persecutions of the next century. Although the Romans refused Jews access to Jerusalem and Jews ceased to live in the southern part of the country, Jewish life flourished in the Galilee, where Jews were the majority of the population. With Rome's conversion to Christianity in the mid fourth century, the lot of the Jews in Palestine became much more difficult and thousands emigrated, particularly to Babylonia. By the early fifth century, Christians were the majority in the Land; by the early seventh century, the number of Jewish settlements was reduced to about 50, and the Jews constituted 10 to 15 percent of the total population.[22]

The end of Christian rule in the Holy Land brought an improvement in the conditions of Jewish life. Small numbers of Jews living elsewhere in the Muslim world migrated there to enjoy the spiritual benefits of dwelling in the Land, which again became an important center of Jewish learning and scholarship. Scholars in Tiberias fixed the vocalization of the Hebrew Bible (the Massoretic text) between the eighth and tenth centuries, while Jerusalem became an important intellectual and religious center in the tenth and eleventh centuries, with both rabbinic and Karaite academies of stature. The Crusades interrupted this period of growth, destroying almost entirely the Jewries of Jerusalem, Caesarea, Haifa, Ramleh, and Jaffa. When the Spanish-Jewish traveler Benjamin of Tudela visited the country in about 1165, he found that the academy of Jerusalem had been transferred to Damascus and that the Jewish population of that city (about three thousand persons) was larger than that of the whole Land of Israel. Yet the village communities in the Galilee survived, as did the communities of Acco, where Benjamin counted about two hundred Jews, and Ashkelon, where he found the same number.[23]

The restoration of Muslim control at the end of the twelfth century did not reverse dramatically the conditions for Jewish settlement, and, in general, Palestine remained a harsh and dangerous place for Jews to live until the late nineteenth century. Political instability, economic decline, and administrative neglect and mismanagement, as well as persecution, combined to keep the size of the Jewish population small over the long run. Yet the flow of Jewish immigrants—scholars, mystics, ordinary pious folk, refugees from Christian intolerance—never dried up and remained sufficient to replenish the existing community. In the sixteenth century in particular, the Land of Israel became a refuge for Iberian Jewish exiles, with the Jewish population reaching approximately 10,000 at midcentury.[24] Safed in the Upper Galilee developed into both a commercial center for the weaving and preparation of woolens and a spiritual center for some of the most original and profound mystics in Jewish history, chief of whom were Isaac Luria (1534-72) and his disciple Hayyim Vital (1543-1620).[25] At the beginning of the seventeenth century, Safed had 300 rabbinic scholars, 18 schools, 21 synagogues, and a large academy with 100 students and 20 teachers. But Turkish mismanagement, Bedouin and Druze incursions, disease, and natural disasters reduced the community to only 50 families by 1764.[26]

While the Land of Israel was never without a Jewish settlement at any time, those Jews who returned there from the Diaspora were relatively few. As the prominent German scholar Rabbi Jacob Emden (1697-1776) hyperbolically observed, "Not one in a thousand fared forth to settle there, perhaps only one from a whole country, and two out of a whole generation."[27] Why this should have been so may seem at first something of a mystery, given the centrality of the Land of Israel in the religion of the Jews. After all, it might reasonably be asked, if the spiritual benefits of living in the Holy Land were so great, why did so few Jews make the effort to live there, particularly since there was no time when they were forbidden absolutely to do so? Undoubtedly, pragmatic considerations had much to do with keeping the number of immigrants low. The journey was expensive and hazardous, the Christian and Muslim overlords were hostile, political conditions were unstable, and the land was poor, not readily yielding a living. (Most Jews who settled there in the centuries before Zionist resettlement depended on charity funds collected abroad.) Equally critical were the attachments of Diaspora Jews to family and friends and to the lands where they had grown up. However frequently and fervently they prayed for their speedy restoration to the Land, they undoubtedly felt at the same time that exile was not always bitter and that the lands where they dwelled were home in one way or another. After all, material comfort and political security were not unknown in the premodern Jewish world. In the West, Spanish, Polish, and Italian Jewries all enjoyed "golden ages" at various times. In these periods of tranquility and prosperity, Emden wrote, "No heart longed for its (the Land's) love or was concerned with its welfare, and no one yearned to behold it. When we found a little rest, we thought we had come upon a new Land of Israel and a new Jerusalem."[28]

There was a countervailing theological doctrine that also worked to check Jewish migration to the Holy Land. The standard rabbinic explanation of Israel's dispersion was that the Exile was divinely ordained as punishment for disobedience. National restoration was in God's hands; he would bring the Exile to an end in his own good time. Thus, human efforts to alter what God had arranged were usually regarded as impious (except, of course, in moments of messianic enthusiasm). From this perspective, ironically, living in exile could be viewed as the natural course for Jews, since it was precisely what God had ordained for them—at least in the short run. (In the ultimate scheme of things, it was regarded as unnatural and temporary.) No serious reevaluation of this doctrine of exile occurred until the appearance of Zionism with its secular political orientation, which attributed the dispersion to mundane historical circumstances that could be overcome by merely human efforts.

Both doctrinally and emotionally, however, the Land of Israel remained central to the religious consciousness of Jews everywhere. Only in Western Europe and North America in the period between the French Revolution and the Nazi regime did substantial groups of Jews deny that the fate of the Jews was bound up with the Land of Israel. Their rejection of this doctrine was part of a larger transformation in self-identity that accompanied Jewish emancipation in the West.[29] In all periods of Jewish history prior to the late eighteenth century, Jews lived as a distinct corporate body with a large measure of internal legal autonomy. Their Judaism was an all-embracing civilization, a way of life, a point of orientation by which to measure all other activities and values. They did not think of themselves as members of the groups in whose midst they dwelled but as members of the Jewish people or nation. As Jews in the West sought or gained political equality and exchanged many of the habits of traditional Jewish life for the mores of the states where they lived, a shift occurred in their sense of personal identity. They ceased to define themselves exclusively in Jewish terms. Jewishness became only a part of their sense of self. They remained Jews in most cases, but also became Englishmen, Frenchmen, Germans, and Americans. Their Jewish identity lost its national component and became, in their view, largely a religious category. To use a now discredited formula, they believed themselves to be Germans or Frenchmen of the Mosaic faith. In those states where gentile opposition to emancipation was strong, Jews worked to reduce their national distinctiveness by reforming Jewish beliefs and practices. They sought to show that they no longer constituted a separate national group living in exile and hoping for restoration to Jerusalem. They insisted that their future was in the states where they lived, not in the Middle East. The 1818 prayer book of the Hamburg Temple, one of the first Reform synagogues in Europe, did not speak of a messiah who would lead the Jews back to the Holy Land but of a universal God who would send redemption to Israel and all mankind.[30] Abraham Geiger, the leading personality in the development of Reform Judaism in nineteenth-century Germany, was quite explicit: for the Jews of his time, Jerusalem was "an entirely indifferent city [and] nothing more than a venerable ruin, a decayed knight's castle." To pray for its welfare was "vain, a romantic phase." The only reason that Jews had hoped for a messiah to return them to Palestine was that they had had no fatherland in Europe.[31] With emancipation, the leaders of assimilationist Jewry believed that they had found acceptance and security. The Exile had come to an end.

The denigration of Zion by the assimilated Jewries of the West was a short-lived phase in Jewish history lasting barely a century and a half—from the early nineteenth century until World War II (short-lived, that is, within the context of three thousand years of Jewish history). Its appeal was limited as well. It made few inroads into Eastern Europe, where the great bulk of Europe's Jews lived, or into North Africa and the Middle East, where ancient, unwesternized communities still clung to traditional hopes for messianic redemption. Only a handful of Eastern European Jews—socialists, intellectuals, industrialists, bankers, and contractors—thought that Russia or Poland was their Zion, Petersburg or Warsaw their Jerusalem.

In both Western and Eastern Europe, the rise of anti-Semitic movements at the turn of the century and their culmination in the Holocaust restored the Land of Israel to a position of prominence in Jewish consciousness. The outbreak of the Jewish question in Europe in the 1870s and its ubiquitous presence in political and cultural life through the 1930s gave birth to Zionism, which came to reject both the assimilationist ideology of Western Jewry and the political passivity of traditional Jewry regarding their fate. Zionism accepted the anti-Semitic contention that the Jews were strangers incapable of being absorbed into the European states and maintained as well, contrary to assimilationist claims, that the Jews were a distinct people, their bonds primarily national and only secondarily religious. Zionism also viewed the Jewish future in Europe pessimistically, arguing that only in the Land of Israel, renewed and rebuilt by human hands, would the Jews find security and dignity.

Zionism attracted relatively few Jews to its standard before the triumph of Nazism. Only then, in the 1930s and 1940s, with history lending credence to its claims, did Zionism cease to be a minority viewpoint. After the war, as the scope of the Holocaust became known to the surviving Jews of Europe and the United States and the struggle to create a Jewish state unfolded before them, Palestine reasserted its hold on Jewish communities everywhere in the Diaspora. The establishment of the state itself and the wars of 1956, 1967, and 1973 further refocussed Jewish attention on the Land—to the extent that knowledge of and concern for Israel in the communities of the Diaspora are greater today than at any time in the past.

Of course, the character of Diaspora Jewry's concern with the Land of Israel—or, better, the state of Israel—differs markedly from what it was in earlier centuries. Given the essentially secular nature of the modern world, few Diaspora Jews wait for the messiah to transport them to a utopian future in the state of Israel or believe that their prayers have greater efficacy in Jerusalem than in New York or Los Angeles. Most Jews today are too far removed from the piety of previous generations to view the Land as sacred territory (although many probably still believe that God promised the Land to the Jews as an eternal inheritance). Yet it would not be incorrect to claim that Jews of various outlooks see the recreation of a Jewish commonwealth as an act of salvation—not salvation as the rabbis of antiquity and the medieval world understood the term, but salvation in a more secular sense. Just as premodern Jews dreamed of a messianic future in which they would return in triumph and glory to their own land, so too the Jews of the West in the past two centuries have yearned for liberation from the insecurities and humiliations of being a despised minority. Some thought that emancipation and assimilation would bring them release; others pinned their hopes on democratic socialism and communism, believing they would create a society in which religious and national divisions would cease to have any significance. Still others gave up all hope and converted to Christianity. For Diaspora Jews in the second half of this century, the state of Israel represents Jewish liberation from Christian and Muslim domination and Jewish victory over a hostile world. Whether or not Jews from Europe and the United States choose to settle in the state of Israel, they still derive psychological comfort and satisfaction from its existence. Although this form of salvation hardly approximates the rabbinic view of Israel's messianic future, it nevertheless functions in the same way, offering hope and consolation to Jews who might otherwise feel overwhelmed by the tragic course of much of Jewish history in the twentieth century.

NOTES

1. Eretz Yisrael ("the Land of Israel") is the traditional Hebrew term for the territory known as the Holy Land in the Christian world. In Hebrew texts, it is frequently referred to simply as ha-aretz ("the Land").

2. James Parkes develops this perspective at length, although from a different viewpoint than my own, in pt. 2 of his Whose Land? A History of the Peoples of Palestine, rev. ed. (Harmondsworth, Middlesex: Penguin Books, 1970).

3. For an exhaustive exploration of this theme in the early history of Christianity, see W. D. Davies, The Gospel and the Land: Early Christianity and Jewish Territorial Doctrine (Berkeley and Los Angeles: University of California Press, 1974).

4. See ibid., pt. 1, "The Land in Israelite Religion and Judaism."

5. Gen. 13:14-17.

6. On the history of Jewish messianism, see the following: Abba Hillel Silver, A History of Messianic Speculation in Israel (Boston: Beacon Press, Beacon Paperback ed., 1959); Gerson D. Cohen, Messianic Postures of Ashkenazim and Sephardim (Prior to Sabbethai Zevi), Leo Baeck Memorial Lecture 9 (New York: Leo Baeck Institute, 1967); Gershom Scholem, "Toward an Understanding of the Messianic Idea in Judaism" and "The Crisis of Tradition in Jewish Messianism," in The Messianic Idea in Judaism and Other Essays in Jewish Spirituality (New York: Schocken Books, 1971); and Aaron Zev Aescoly, Ha-tenuot ha-meshihiyyot be-Yisrael: otzer ha-mekorot ve-ha-teudot le-toldot ha-meshihiyyut be-Yisrael [Jewish messianic movements: sources and documents on messianism in Jewish history] (Jerusalem: Mosad Bialik, 1956).

7. Raphael Patai has collected and translated into English a wide variety of texts about the coming of the messiah and the messianic age. See his The Messiah Texts (Detroit: Wayne State University Press, 1979). See also the collection of apocalyptic messianic writings edited by Yehudah Ibn Shmuel, Midreshei ha-geulah [Legends of redemption], rev. ed. (Jerusalem: Mosad Bialik, 1954).

8. "Mishneh Torah," in Isadore Twersky, ed., A Maimonides Reader (New York: Behrman House, 1972), pp. 224-26.

9. For numerous examples of liturgical references to Jerusalem, see Avraham Holtz, The Holy City: Jews on Jerusalem (New York: W. W. Norton, 1971), pp. 100-10.

10. Herman Pollack, Jewish Folkways in Germanic Lands (1648-1806): Studies in Aspects of Daily Life (Cambridge, Mass.: MIT Press, 1971), pp. 29-30, 106.

11. Gerson D. Cohen, "Zion in Rabbinic Literature," in Zion in Jewish Literature, ed. Abraham S. Halkin (New York: Herzl Press, 1961), pp. 38-64.

12. Pirkei de Rabbi Eliezer 35, quoted in Holtz, The Holy City, p. 74.

13. The translation is that of David Goldstein, from his fine anthology The Jewish Poets of Spain, 900-1250, rev. ed. (Harmondsworth, Middlesex: Penguin Books, 1971), p. 128.

14. On Yehudah Ha-Levi's longing for Zion, see Yitzhak F. Baer, *Galut*, trans. Robert Warshow (New York: Schocken Books, 1947), pp. 27-35.

15. Yehudah Ha-Levi, *Kuzari*, bk. 5, par. 23, in *Three Jewish Philosophers*, ed. and trans. Isaak Heinemann (New York: Harper & Row, Harper Torchbook ed., 1965), pp. 126-27.

16. Ibid., par. 25, pp. 127-28.

17. Salo Wittmayer Baron, *A Social and Religious History of the Jews*, 2d ed., rev., 17 vols. to date (New York: Columbia University Press, 1952-), 5: 184.

18. Ibid., pp. 202-4. David Alroy became the subject of an historical novel by Benjamin Disraeli, *The Wondrous Tale of Alroy*, published in 1833.

19. See Gershom Scholem's magisterial account, *Sabbatai Sevi: The Mystical Messiah, 1626-1676* (Princeton, N.J.: Princeton University Press, 1973).

20. Beth-Zion Abrahams, ed. and trans., *The Life of Glückel of Hameln, 1646-1724* (London: East and West Library, 1962), p. 46.

21. There is no single volume that traces the continuity of Jewish settlement in the Land of Israel. The following specialized accounts are helpful: Michael Avi-Yonah, *The Jews of Palestine: A Political History from the Bar Kochba War to the Arab Conquest* (Oxford: Basil Blackwell, 1976); Joshua Prawer, *The Latin Kingdom of Jerusalem: European Colonialism in the Middle Ages* (London: Weidenfeld and Nicolson, 1972), chap. 13; and Yitzhak Ben-Zvi, *Eretz Yisrael vi-yeshuvah bi-yemei ha-shilton ha-Otomani* [The Land of Israel in the period of Ottoman rule], 2d ed. (Jerusalem: Mosad Bialik, 1966). A greatly abridged English translation of the work by Ben-Zvi appeared as "Eretz Yisrael under Ottoman Rule, 1517-1917," in *The Jews: Their History, Culture, and Religion*, ed. Louis Finkelstein, 3d ed., 2 vols. (Philadelphia: Jewish Publication Society, 1966), 1: 602-89.

22. Avi-Yonah, *The Jews of Palestine*, pp. 19, 220, 241.

23. Marcus Nathan Adler, ed. and trans., *The Itinerary of Benjamin of Tudela* (New York: Philipp Feldheim, n.d.), pp. 19, 22, 28, 30.

24. Norman A. Stillman, *The Jews of Arab Lands: A History and Source Book* (Philadelphia: Jewish Publication Society, 1979), p. 89.

25. On Safed as a center of mysticism, see Solomon Schechter, "Safed in the Sixteenth Century—A City of Legists and Mystics," in his *Studies in Judaism*, 2d ser. (Philadelphia: Jewish Publication Society, 1908); and R. J. Zwi Werblowsky, *Joseph Karo: Lawyer and Mystic*, 2d ed. (Philadelphia: Jewish Publication Society, 1977), chap. 4, "Spiritual Life in Sixteenth-Century Safed: Mystical and Magical Contemplation."

26. Encyclopaedia Judaica, s.v. "Safed."

27. Jacob Emden, Bet Yaakov [The house of Jacob] (Lvov, Russia, 1901), intro., quoted in In Time and Eternity: A Jewish Reader, ed. Nahum N. Glatzer (New York: Schocken Books, 1946), pp. 216-17.

28. Ibid.

29. On the origins of Jewish modernity in Western Europe, see Jacob Katz, Out of the Ghetto: The Social Background of Jewish Emancipation, 1770-1870 (Cambridge, Mass.: Harvard University Press, 1973); for a very different perspective, see Todd M. Endelman, The Jews of Georgian England, 1714-1830: Tradition and Change in a Liberal Society (Philadelphia: Jewish Publication Society, 1979).

30. Michael A. Meyer, The Origins of the Modern Jew: Jewish Identity and European Culture in Germany, 1749-1824 (Detroit: Wayne State University Press, 1967), p. 136.

31. Abraham Geiger, "Etwas über Glauben und Beten: Zu Schutz und Trutz," Jüdische Zeitschrift für Wissenschaft und Leben 7 (1869): 52-54, quoted in Jakob J. Petuchowski, Prayerbook Reform in Europe: The Liturgy of European Liberal and Reform Judaism (New York: World Union for Progressive Judaism, 1968), p. 280.

2

REQUIREMENTS FOR A STABLE PEACE: ARAB AND ISRAELI IMAGES

ABDUL AZIZ SAID
ALAIN SPORTICHE

"Appearances to the mind are (of) four kinds," wrote Epictetus centuries ago. "Things either are what they appear to be; or they neither are, nor appear to be; or they are and do not appear to be; or they are not, and yet appear to be. Rightly to aim in all these is the wise man's task."[1] And because "wars begin in the minds of individuals, it is in the minds of individuals that the defenses of peace must be constructed."[2] The Arab-Israeli conflict may be partially explained by the roles of images, beliefs, cognitive maps, and values. The understanding of the psychological barriers separating both groups may lead to the discovery of a commonality of images, the beginning of dispassionate negotiations, and the building of a stable relationship.

The purpose of this chapter is threefold: first, to describe individual behaviors such as prejudice and distance; second, to explain the development of images and their receptivity to change; and third, to assess our predictive capabilities.

In international relations, social psychology focuses upon the psychology of individual behavior, the sociology of institutional processes, and the interaction between these two fields of study.[3] It deals with individual attitudes and motives in an international situation and examines the relationships between them. Kenneth Boulding has put it aptly: "It is what we think the world is like, not what it is really like, that determines our behavior."[4] Actors' behavior depends upon their image of the environment, their perception of external reality, and the influence of appearance upon the actors. Knowledge of the environment is subjective, and facts are perceived according to the meaning ascribed to them by the interpreter. Information is thus selective and sensitive. A new reality emerges from the original facts. Individuals react to appearances rather than to reality. They build a fictitious world with all its stimulus-response consequences.

Boulding explains, "There are no such things as facts. There are only messages filtered through a changeable value system."[5] Facts do not speak for themselves. Individuals use facts to express their own preferences and perceptions. Perception includes three components: value—what ought to be as opposed to what is and what marks preferences; belief—an analytical proposition describing and assuming reality as true; and cognition—the information received from the environment.

What occurs is a reaction to our image of the world; image, in this context, acts as both a dependent and independent variable—being affected and affecting.[6] A new cognitive map of the nation is held that redefines itself and the world. The image that has no basis in reality creates a different, distorted reality that is interpreted as true. William Isaac Thomas has expressed this effectively: "If men define situations as real, they are real in their consequences."[7] Assumptive behavior creates a counterbehavior, and when reality disappears the image only produces a counterimage.

Struggles are perceived in a context of imagery and illusion. Selectivity produces distorted perceptions and creates new ideological stereotype images. When individuals hear what they expect to hear, the images do not match reality and resist change. Images that are important in shaping a "proper" view of a situation do not necessarily serve as a basis for trends or prediction. Dual incorrect perception combined with dual inaccurate analysis jeopardizes long-range cooperative behavior.[8] Mirror image undermines cooperation and enhances communication failure, thus leading to an escalatory process. Frank and Weisband assert, "The way two states see each other frequently affects the way they interact. A pattern of systematic cooperation is not likely to develop between states that perceive each other as evil, aggressive and immoral."[9] Each side (actor) assumes its righteousness and describes the other as the sin carrier. Competition masks similarities, leads to suspicion, increases hostility, destroys communication, and supports a Manichaean view of the world. George Kennan wrote more than a quarter of a century ago, "It is an undeniable privilege of every man to prove himself right in the thesis that the world is his enemy; for if he reiterates it frequently enough and makes it the background of his conduct, he is bound eventually to be right."[10]

The national belief system contains long-range unchanging images, remains stable, and is not easily affected by change. Deep values resist contradiction by dissonant cognition.[11] Boulding writes, "When [the image] receives messages which conflict with it, its first impulse is to reject them as in some sense being untrue."[12] The national perceptual framework survives challenges presented by new experiences. It requires much more than superficial improvements to adjust to new realities. Janis and Smith observe, "Attempts at producing changes in social or political prejudices and stereotypes generally meet with an extraordinarily high degree of psychological resistance . . . will be met by strong resistance . . . at each step of the . . . process."[13] Deutsch and Merritt confirm that fundamental changes require more time: "Almost nothing in the world seems to be able to shift the images of forty per cent of the population in most countries, even within one or two decades. Combinations of events that shift the images and attitudes even of the remaining fifty or sixty per cent of the population are extremely rare."[14]

Ralph White found six images of nations in conflict: (1) diabolical enemy image (amoral), (2) virile self-image (status and prestige, as opposed to humiliation), (3) moral self-image (wholly good versus bad motives), (4) absence of empathy (no capacity to view a situation from the perspective of other people), (5) selective inattention (sustaining perceptions that ignore others), and (6) military overconfidence.[15]

Werner Levi advises us to "try to discover . . . these missing elements whose presence leads to the avoidance of the use of violence."[16] It is also possible to use cooperation to reach one's objectives. By increasing similarities, developing common interests, reducing differences, and avoiding a black and white picture, violence can be stopped. Dina Zinnes remarks, "When there is no perception of hostility, there is no expression of hostility, but when hostility is perceived it is replied to with hostility."[17] Negotiations and bargaining replace limited objectives and unhealthy prejudices. A commonality of goals once established may produce beneficial outcomes for both parties. This may open the way for cross-national contacts, educate public opinion, reintroduce a balanced image, liquidate stereotypes, and reform attitudes.

The emergence of the state of Israel is the institutionalization of a group religious faith into a state lacking security and nationalism. It is the product of Jewish experience and history and consequently carries its heritage, whose essence rests upon the following assumptions: Jews depend only on themselves; Jews are an unwanted element in the world; and Jews have to provide themselves with physical, social, and intellectual strength to survive in a hostile environment.

Israeli policies are oriented toward security and survival. Security provides the strength to survive as a Jewish state. Israel still carries the traditional Jewish aspiration of "Next Year in Jerusalem." Jewish survival develops loyalty to other Jews and is reflected in an intense emotional attachment to the land and the people, to the country and an integrated population. Lack of trust and suspicion of others dominate. This prevents the temptation to change, for any change may lead to the final catastrophe.

The Arabs have been misruled for centuries by local ruling elites and foreign powers. They have developed a feeling of humiliation as a result of perceived colonialism. Traditional loyalties to the family, tribe, group, and Arab nation (ummah) remain strong. These sentiments contradict the nation-state and underscore conformity and authoritarianism. Social pressure controls actions and promotes conformity. A transitional society with changing institutions is suspicious of others.

The Israelis perceive a threat to their security and survival. Any information contradicting this belief creates cognitive dissonance, and the information is distorted, denied, or rejected. Paradoxically the Israelis have adopted a new concept, that the only chance for the Arabs is peace; Arabs need peace and must seek it.

As for the Arabs, Israelis are regarded as intruders in the Arab nation. Their presence is an affront to the Arabs and is indefensible, diplomatically and legally. Israel is considered a constant military threat to their security, unity, and development. In addition to their humiliation by the Europeans, the Arabs see themselves paying for a century of anti-Semitism. The frustration of their injured dignity and challenged honor leaves no other choice but war. Hisham Sharabi captures the sense of Arab dignity: "Dignity is implicit in being truly independent and sovereign. For Arabs, it represents one of the highest values on the personal as well as the collective levels. For the individual it sums up the totality of his worth as a man. It manifests itself not merely in bearing or in external form of conduct; it consists primarily in a subjective sense of self-esteem —to lose dignity is to lose self-respect."[18]

Israel is alien to the Third World and is therefore associated with colonialism and imperialism, which hinders Arab aspirations. Israel is integrated with the West and is thus a member of the wrong camp in the struggle to recapture a denied superiority. Security in the Land clashes with sovereignty over the Land. Israel security is threatened by decreasing sovereignty, partition, and Palestinian demography.

The struggle may be analyzed within the context of game theory: a zero-sum game for the Israelis, to be or not to be; for the Arabs, a non-zero-sum game to recover their land. Israeli presence and occupation of the land means defense and increased deterrence. Time becomes a dynamic concept associated with life. Israel defends its territory through two different means: (1) material means, achieved through dissuasion and military force, and (2) psychological means, a more classic form of struggle (that is, politics). But Israel hides the question of to be or not to be.

To the Arabs, Israel is an ideological, racial, non-Arab sovereignty occupying Arab land. Islamic Arab sovereignty is challenged by _dhimmis_ ("enthusiasts") who have to be protected. Islam embraces cultural diversity but denies political coexistence in its sphere of sovereignty. In the Arab view, Israeli presence is creating a geopolitical disequilibrium. This transforms the game for the Arabs into a zero-sum game. Any defeat enhances the status quo, which perpetuates Israeli expansion. There is no other choice than to contemplate the game in its totality; that is, the destruction of Israel. It is no longer a classic war, but a perpetual, everlasting one. The stake is "nothing but all" as opposed to "to be or not to be." There remains no solution.

The limited opportunities of contact between Arabs and Israelis protect stereotype perceptions. Images remain unclear since both use a mirror image. The other is wrong, the aggressor, and I am right. The Arabs are right and the Israelis are right. The two rights are clashing.

For Israel, no military victory can solve the essence of its problem, no field success can assure its right to existence. For the Arabs, any defeat is a nonvictory for the Israelis. How could the four components of the conflict be resolved: an ideologico-racial antagonism for the same land, differences in psychological attitudes and social behavior, anti-imperialism versus western liberalism and the related problems of economic development, and supremacy of the nation over the individual? Image analysis applied to the Middle East conflict describes an environment charged with hostility. Changes are difficult. A better understanding of the components of the conflict may bring us closer to a dispassionate approach. An awareness of commonalities undermines the superstructures and may lead to a common image. This may be realized in decreased perceptual errors and maximized sympathy. Possibilities exist that may increase communication between adversaries. Attitudinal changes require patience and goodwill. Areas of agreement should be commonly explored. Role reversal in restating the other position may bring correct bargaining closer to fruition. Mediators who are able to listen and understand both parties may be precious. Both actors can be inspired by their rich traditions. The highly praised people of the Book may help Ismael to secure his identity, and Ismael may help Israel to secure its existence. The Arab people of the Land of Revelation may see the light upon their path.

Much has changed since the war of 1948. Pan-Arabism and Zionism have been costly; they have been betrayed by their own vague goals of victory. The wars demonstrably narrowed the strategic distance between them technologically as well as in a perceptual sense. Until recently, Arabs and Israelis had little relations, and neither side knew quite what to do with the other. Their goals were imprecise. While both were explicit about the utopias they sought, they were vague about goals: victory, peace, and security.

REQUIREMENTS FOR A STABLE PEACE / 23

There is a new generation and a new perception in the Arab world and Israel. Earlier Arabs and Israelis were landlocked by faulty perceptions. Israelis chose to believe the worst of Arab statements, and Arabs interpreted Zionism in its worst light.

Traditionally, the Israelis did not see themselves as another Middle Eastern community but rather shared the values and attitudes of Europe and the West. They sought, moreover, to assert their cultural supremacy. The Israelis insisted that they provided the West with the first line of defense vis-à-vis its adversaries, and the Arabs perceived the same.

Four wars have brought Arab and Israeli into closer, if uncomfortable, juxtaposition. During the 1967 war, Israel sought to impress its legitimacy upon the Arabs. In the war of 1973, the Arabs demonstrated to Israel that it cannot impose its will upon them. The resulting stalemate has allowed Arabs and Israelis to perceive themselves in if not quite a win situation, then at least in a no lose situation. This perception of mutual advantage has made the present steps toward peace possible.

Any renewal of hostilities would destroy this present condition of mutual advantage. No country in the Middle East is strong enough to risk this circumstance. Israeli and Arab extremists notwithstanding, the United States and Soviet Union are not willing to risk war for any shaky advantage.

These changes are transforming the conflict from one of people —Arabs and Jews—to one between political entities. The former view carries with it the threat of annihilation of one party to the conflict by the other. The latter perception holds the promise of reconciliation of conflicting interests. The great and glaring fact of the Arab-Israeli conflict today is that an era has ended. National interest is replacing messianism as a foreign policy context. The Arabs, albeit reluctantly, recognize the fact of the existence of Israel. The Israeli claim of omnipotence has become a historical curiosity.

Not everyone is equally sensitive to the new reality. There are certain Arabs and Israelis who insist that no real change has taken place. There are other Arabs and Israelis who, while recognizing the evidence of their senses, are emotionally unable to act on their conclusions. Actually, Arabs and Israelis have no other viable choice but to live with the new reality. The Arab-Israeli conflict is no longer "normal"; it has lost its political meaning and has become pathological. It is important to protect oneself against external dangers, but it is foolish to make this one's primary purpose in life.

The realization of a stable peace requires courage to see the totality, rather than isolated parts. The right image of peace requires Israeli recognition that security depends as much on mental flexibility as it does on military might. It also calls for Arab recognition that dignity is as much self-esteem as it is self-restraint. In the pursuit of survival, those who ponder security problems cannot become enamored with their options. Both Arabs and Israelis must accept limitations on their respective national ambitions. The old strategy of tightrope walking has been a monumental exercise in futility.

NOTES

1. Epictetus *Discoursis* 27.
2. Preamble to the constitution of the United Nations Educational, Scientific and Cultural Organization.
3. Herbert Kelman, "Social-Psychological Approaches: Definition of Scope," in *International Behavior*, ed. Herbert Kelman (New York: Holt Winston, 1965), p. 9.
4. Kenneth Boulding, "National Images and International Systems," in *International Politics and Foreign Policy*, ed. James Rosenau (New York: Free Press, 1969), p. 423.
5. Kenneth Boulding, *The Image* (Ann Arbor: University of Michigan Press, 1956), p. 4.
6. Kelman, "Social-Psychological Approaches," p. 27.
7. William Isaac Thomas and Dorothy S. Thomas, *The Child in America: Behavior Problems and Programs* (New York: Knopf, 1928).
8. Urie Bronfenbrenner, "The Mirror Image in Soviet-American Relations," *Journal of Social Issues*, vol. 27, no. 3 (1961).
9. Thomas Franck and Edward Weisband, *World Politics: Verbal Strategy among the Superpowers* (New York: Oxford University Press, 1972), pp. 151-52.
10. George Kennan (X), "The Sources of the Soviet Conduct," *Foreign Affairs*, July 1947, p. 569.
11. Leon Festinger, *A Theory of Cognitive Dissonance* (Evanston, Ill.: Row Peterson, 1957); Holsti, "Cognitive Dynamics and Images of the Enemy," in *Image and Reality in World Politics*, ed. John C. Farrell and Asa P. Smith (New York: Columbia University Press, 1967); and Robert Jervis, "Consistency in Foreign Policy Views," in *Communication in International Politics*, ed. Richard Merritt (Urbana: University of Illinois Press, 1972).
12. Boulding, *The Image*, p. 8.
13. Irving Janis and Brewster Smith, "Effects of Education and Persuasion on National and International Images," in Kelman, *International Behavior*, pp. 195-96.
14. Karl Deutsch and Richard Merritt, "Effects of Events on National and International Images," in Kelman, *International Behavior*, p. 183.

15. Ralph White, Nobody Wanted War (New York: Doubleday, 1970).

16. Werner Levi, "On the Causes of War and the Conditions of Peace," Journal of Conflict Resolution, Dec. 1960, p. 418.

17. Dina Zinnes, Joseph Zinnes, and Robert McClure, "Hostility in Diplomatic Communication: A Study of the 1916 Crisis," in International Crisis, ed. Charles F. Herman (New York: Free Press, 1972), p. 160.

18. Hisham Sharabi, Nationalism and Revolution in the Arab World (New York: D. Van Nostrand, 1966), p. 98.

3

CHANGE IN THE MIDDLE EAST: IS THERE A CHANCE FOR PEACE?

HAIM SHAKED

In March 1981 people in the Middle East celebrated the second anniversary of the signing of the Israeli-Egyptian peace treaty. November 1981 marked the celebration of the fourth anniversary of President Sadat's historical trip to Jerusalem. It is remarkable that just two years after the peace agreement, almost four years after President Sadat's trip to Jerusalem, quite a few leaders, analysts, and commentators within and without the Middle East seem to be taking these events for granted. What is worse, some would even go so far as to treat the Camp David accords and the peace treaty that followed in its wake as one of the greater calamities afflicting the Middle East in recent history. Whenever they make an analysis of the situation in the region, they tend to emphasize the negative, risky, and disruptive aspects of these agreements and their immediate political and strategic consequences.

It is my basic argument in this chapter that the Israeli-Egyptian peace is a major constructive event, a qualitative leap forward in contemporary Middle Eastern history, perhaps equaled in its significance only by the establishment of independent Middle Eastern states in the mid-1980s. It is my contention that this peace agreement should be regarded as a beginning, which portends a tremendous politico-strategic potential. It should neither be taken for granted, nor should any serious analysis of the current complexities in the Middle East overlook its brighter sides.

Why is it so? What is the main significance of the peace treaty and the process of normalization of relations between Israel and Egypt that it has triggered? Oftentimes, the emergence of peace from a conflict situation is misconstrued and mistakenly defined as tantamount to the cessation of hostilities or the termination of warfare. This perception does not do justice to the true meaning or significance of peace. Peace is not the mirror image of war. Rather, it is a completely different substance; it is an entity unto itself, with its own dynamics. For a number of reasons, this is particularly true in the Middle East.

The Egyptian-Israeli treaty and its continuing gradual implementation bear testimony to the fact that the unpredictable actually came to be a reality. Over the last thirty years or so, the conventional wisdom expressed by numerous specialists in many a conference on the Middle East was that in our generation peace was not possible between Israel and any part of the Arab world. Defying all such predictions and the learned explanations of their inevitability, the impossible did actually happen. Why, then, would it be unreasonable to assume that if a change of such an order of magnitude could take place, others might also occur?

Second, the Israeli-Egyptian peace introduced an element of normalcy into one area of the Arab-Israeli conflict. For almost one hundred years—if one starts the history of the Arab-Israeli conflict from 1882—and particularly so since the war of 1948, the Arab-Israeli conflict contained a major complicating attribute. This attribute, which almost turned the conflict into a sui generis situation, has been the asymmetry between the conflicting parties, as exemplified by the fact that the mainstream of Arab nationalist ideology negated the very legitimacy of Zionism, whereas the mainstream of Zionist ideology sought an accommodation with the other side, never denying the very legitimacy of Arab nationalism. For the first time in a hundred years, the Egyptian-Israeli accord has profoundly altered this particular attribute of the Middle Eastern scene. It has turned the conflict between Israel and Egypt into a normal dispute between two states that disagree over many important aspects of the assessment of, and solution for, the Middle Eastern situation. Nevertheless, it is a dispute between two political entities that mutually recognize each other's existence as a fully sovereign state. This recognition, that all protagonists in this tragic play are legitimate, constitutes the first prerequisite for a more comprehensive and profound change in the future of the Arab-Israeli conflict. Furthermore, it introduces the logic of a political solution into a situation in which, for a number of generations, the protagonists thought of the use of force as the only way to deal with the other side.

A third significance of the Israeli-Egyptian peace treaty is inherent in the fact that it incorporates and balances two basic ingredients of the Egyptian and the Israeli psyches. The first is that there are some very basic attributes of peoples and their states that cannot be skirted or disposed of. In the formula that produced the Egyptian-Israeli peace treaty, Egyptian feelings about the Sinai peninsula, which they claimed back in its entirety, were the equivalent of Israeli feelings about security, which in their eyes was tantamount to the establishment of a bilateral peace, straight and simple. The second was Egypt's recognition of Israel's legitimate claim to sovereignty within the wider Middle Eastern context. Israel's quid pro quo was the incorporation into the Camp David <u>Framework for Peace in the Middle East</u> of two highly important—but unfortunately often overlooked—references to the Palestinian issue: that "the representatives of the Palestinian <u>people</u> should participate in negotiations on the resolutions of the Palestinian <u>problem in all its aspects</u>" and that "the solution from the negotiations must also recognize <u>the legitimate rights of the Palestinian people and their just requirements</u>" (emphasis added).

The recognition by Israel and Egypt alike that peace can come about only through a very delicate formula of mutual recognition of each side's profound sensitivities as well as the application of the principle of compromise to the resolution of their differences was the fourth important attribute of the Israeli-Egyptian agreement. Unfortunately, some major actors in the Middle Eastern situation still adhere to the concept of "all or nothing" that has caused so much trouble and led to so many disasters in the past. As long as this notion prevails, and wherever it exists, not much significant progress can be made toward the extension of peace from a bilateral Israeli-Egyptian arrangement into a more comprehensive Middle Eastern peace.

Finally, a frequently overlooked but important consequence of the Egyptian-Israeli normalization has been the fledgling dialogue that it made possible, not only between leaders and politicians of hitherto enemy states, but also between two peoples of the Middle Eastern region. A famous aphorism defines a monologue as one person talking to himself and a dialogue as two people talking to themselves. The peace between Israel and Egypt provided the first opportunity for the Egyptian and Israeli peoples to talk to each other, to establish direct contact with each other. In the long run, this may turn out to be one of the most important foundations for better understanding and mutual appreciation.

A proper analysis of the Egyptian-Israeli peace and an assessment of its future require an understanding of the factors that caused such a surprising breakthrough. Middle Eastern specialists have been seriously debating this question. To some, the primary factor that made such a change possible is courageous and imaginative leadership. Others maintain that the change should be traced to a convergence of political, economic, military, and cultural circumstances. Without becoming involved in the historiosophical controversy that is implied in this discussion, it could be argued that in this particular case none of the two approaches can on its own provide a full, satisfactory explanation of the Israeli-Egyptian breakthrough. The personalities of President Sadat and Prime Minister Begin, President

Carter, Foreign Minister Dayan, and Defense Minister Weizman have become inseparable components of the Camp David process. The political environment in which they operated, however, cannot be belittled. This environment was shaped by a number of important historical processes. It is an established fact that relative to the 1950s and 1960s, the 1970s were a period of remarkable domestic political stability in the region. Whereas the preceding two decades saw, in most Middle Eastern countries, waves of revolutions and coups d'etat, the 1970s were characterized—except in a few notable cases such as Lebanon and Iran—by continuity of regimes. (Syria is perhaps the best possible example of this remarkable change.) This development was coupled with the diminishing importance of pan-Arab nationalism as a major ideological and political driving force and the rise in the visibility and importance of local patriotism—Syrian, Jordanian, Iraqi, or Egyptian nationalism, and so forth. While the slogans and catchwords of pan-Arab ideology, exemplified in the late 1950s and early 1960s by the messianic impact of Ba'thism and Nasserism, continued throughout the 1970s to be in use by most Arab spokesmen, their meaning was gradually transformed from the operational to the ritualistic. The reality of the existence of separate nation-states thus overpowered the dream of a united Arab nation ruled from one center. This, in turn, created a new Middle East, in the sense that the polycentric composition of the regional mosaic asserted, or rather reasserted, itself and gave rise to a plethora of localized conflicts. For the first time in decades, the Arab-Israeli conflict lost much of its centrality and ubiquitousness within the overall picture of Middle Eastern policies. It was relegated into an important but no longer omnipresent aspect of Middle Eastern life. At times other conflicts, such as the civil war in Lebanon in 1975-76 (or later on, the Iraqi-Iranian war, which erupted in September 1980) even overshadowed, at least for a while, the Arab-Israeli conflict.

Finally, within the socioeconomic sphere, a certain rhythm took its toll. Frustrations that followed the independence of the mid-1940s bred coups d'etat, radicalism, and revolution in the 1950s and early 1960s. But revolution, too, had to fulfill the expectations it raised. Time and mounting difficulties brought about a recognition that the solution of serious domestic shortcomings did not lie in the externalization of the problem, but rather, in internal modernization and development. This, in turn, required an international reorientation: from reliance on the USSR, which could supply little else than armaments and military hardware, toward the West, which could provide both military and significant economic aid and technological know-how. As has been the case with many other significant areas in which Egypt was traditionally the first in the Arab world to introduce change and set an example for the others, in the case of changing regional and international outlooks, too, Egypt assumed a leadership or trailblazing position. There were, however, some more immediate causes for the change of heart in Egypt. The war of 1973 (the Ramadan War to the Arabs, the Yom Kippur War to the Israelis) brought about the realization by President Sadat that even when the elements of surprise and initiative were totally on the Arab side, Israel's military could not only not be destroyed but managed to penetrate Egypt's depth up to a distance of 101 kilometers from Cairo. The steep rise in oil prices following the 1973-74 dramatic change in Organization of Petroleum Exporting Countries (OPEC) policy and the tremendous surpluses that were beginning to accumulate in the coffers of the oil-rich countries in the Middle East helped raise Arab morale, but also—and this is not as well known—further demonstrated that the rulers of OPEC countries were not prepared to share their riches with their poverty-stricken sister Arab countries. The dynamics of the 1974-75 disengagement and separation of forces agreements that Henry Kissinger negotiated enhanced U.S. credibility in the eyes of Middle Eastern leaders and provided a backdrop for the series of events that took place in 1977: the change of a U.S. administration and its abortive attempt to revive the Geneva Conference; the change of government in Israel and the secret negotiations with Egypt that were initiated by the new Begin government in the summer; and the attempt by the United States in early October to reintroduce the USSR as a partner in a Middle Eastern settlement. All these culminated in President Sadat's announcement that he would be willing to travel to Jerusalem and Prime Minister Begin's immediate extension of a formal invitation.

Thus, whether by coincidence or historical predestination, the right leadership was there, at the crossroads of profound processes of change. Furthermore, they were willing to come to grips with the new circumstances. Their assessment that peace between their countries was possible, their conviction that their interests would be served better by pursuit of the path of political negotiations than by treading the war path, and their ability to share these convictions with their peoples paved the way to the Camp David accords and the peace treaty and saved them—at least thus far—from becoming a meaningless piece of paper.

All the above elements contributed to the creation of an opportunity. But the outcome is not devoid of major risks. There is a dark side to this picture that should also not be ignored. The Israeli-Egyptian peace still is, and for a long time will remain, inherently fragile and reversible. Many Israelis have argued, and Egyptians have concurred, that the peace between the two nations is skin deep, and that it has not yet transformed the situation into a solid reality that could withstand internal combustion and external pressures.

Many analysts are agreed that as long as this peace remains an arrangement that binds only two out of all Middle Eastern parties involved in the Arab-Israeli conflict, the polarization of Israel and Egypt, on the one hand, and most Arab countries, on the other, will expose the Israeli-Egyptian accord to grave dangers. One of the most significant developments in the post-Camp David period has been the undeniable feeling of isolation from the rest of the Arab world that prevails among many leading members of the Egyptian intelligentsia. President Sadat may have appeared to many observers as Gulliver in the land of Lilliput (so implied by his reference to objecting Arab leaders as dwarfs). Yet, to some Arab leaders and elites, he was nothing but a shameful traitor. To Israel and Egypt alike, peace has come as a shock. The outbreak of war is an often-used term, but there is also a phenomenon that might best be termed the outbreak of peace, and the shock that it causes requires a painful adjustment. Indeed, the longevity and the complexity of the Arab-Israeli conflict require a rather long time before the two parties concerned can and will adjust to this new situation. In the process, they will continue to be exposed to a number of major unsettling pressures. To many Israelis, peace with Egypt constitutes a dream come true; any awakening with the shattering of their dream will mean a grave psychological disaster. To many Egyptians, peace is a price paid for more important gains; they would not wish to find out that the price was much too high. On both sides of the border, peace and the process that led to its emergence have implanted the seeds of new expectations and have revived old ones. On both sides of the border, too, peace has not obliterated deep suspicions nor arrested an inertia of long-standing violence.

Furthermore, there is no guarantee that processes that created a certain environment in the late 1970s will continue to exist in the 1980s. Domestic stability in the Arab world may be shaken. Quite a few indicators put a very serious question mark over the ability of a number of leading Arab governments to sustain their political power for another decade. Renewed instability might cause great turbulence in one area, and in turn it could suck in other, more remote actors. Messianic pan-Arabism (with or without an Islamic taint) is not, by any yardstick, a dead force, and it might reawaken to produce another wave of major disturbances. The rise of polycentrism in the Arab world has, indeed, produced new and highly localized focuses of crisis, but these, as in the cases of the Persian Gulf and Lebanon, may easily erupt beyond their immediate confines and turn into major forces of disruption of a regional scope. To all of these potential dangers, one might add a number of more acute deficiencies in the post-Camp David process as it has evolved recently. The first could be termed the routinization of future negotiations. The overemphasis on technical and legalistic aspects of the autonomy talks is one, but in no way the only, example in point. It exemplifies an attitude that regards the arrangement agreed upon in Camp David not as a foundation for a new Middle Eastern construction, but as its ceiling.

The second is the continuing procrastination of the United States with its formulation of a clear-cut Middle Eastern policy. The credibility of the United States in the region, which the Carter administration inherited from its predecessor and which was so instrumental in the triggering and shaping of the Camp David process, was very badly battered by the Iranian crisis, including the mishandling of the hostages affair. The first six months of the Reagan administration did not do much to reverse this trend. The initial concentration of the new administration on its external action in El Salvador conveyed, perhaps inadvertently, a message that the Middle East was not high up on the foreign affairs agenda of the United States. The declared attempt to subsume all U.S. assessments and actions to a rather simplified East-West rivalry and competition could not impress Middle Eastern governments, let alone goad them into action. Moreover, the formula of strategic consensus between conflicting Middle Eastern parties, which Secretary of State Haig took with him as his main message on his first Middle Eastern trip in April 1981, had no chance of getting into a new reality in the region unless it was backed up by highly sophisticated and well-coordinated action. It remained to be seen whether once through with its initial domestic economic drive and following the June 30, 1981, elections in Israel, the Reagan administration would come around to a more involved and better performed role in the Middle East. Even so, by the time the new Israeli government was sworn in, the U.S. Congress and president returned from their August vacations, and Egypt and Israel had their first tête-à-tête talks with the United States, many new complicated elements were added to the Middle Eastern picture: the reverberations of the Israeli raid on the nuclear facility in Baghdad; the Syrian-Israeli-Lebanese-Palestine Liberation Organization (PLO) crisis and U.S. mediation; and the proposed sale of highly sophisticated U.S. weapons systems to Saudi Arabia, and the Lebanese crisis of 1982 are but a few examples in point. Last, but not least, the restoration of U.S. credibility and the ability of the United States to assume the initiative in the Middle East were much more difficult in the autumn of 1981 than in the late winter of 1981. The aura of a new U.S. government that moved into Washington on the wave of an incredible landslide election victory and promised to be radically different from its predecessor could not be maintained for too long. Three hundred days after the inauguration of a new president, the glitter becomes tarnished and his ability becomes a matter that has been tested.

What is the balance of the above account? An important ingredient of any long-lasting solution of the Arab-Israeli conflict is not to look back in anger, to recount the endless list of tragic facts that constitute the sad history of Jewish-Arab relations in modern times, or to concentrate on all the woes of the situation and subsequently reach a pessimistic conclusion. Rather, one should concentrate on the positive potentialities of the prevailing conditions without ignoring the great risks involved and the sources of serious danger. The crucial question is how to turn the Egyptian-Israeli peace treaty from a tombstone to Camp David into a cornerstone for a new Middle Eastern construction; how to convert it from a bilateral Egyptian-Israeli arrangement into a more comprehensive platform. It is essential that all parties concerned and interested in furthering peace in the region be prepared to recognize that great urgency is involved, and that at least one other Arab entity has to visibly endorse the process and join in its implementation. Whether this entity should be the Palestinians or an Arab state or whether progress should be sought on both tracks simultaneously is indeed the most pressing operational question in any strategy that would aim at further buttressing and extending the Egyptian-Israeli peace.

The Israeli-Egyptian peace treaty has, in the opinion of the present author, provided all parties involved—Israelis and Palestinians, Syrians and Egyptians, Jordanians and Saudis—with an opportunity that, if maintained, will outweigh the risks. One can only hope that the political leadership of the parties involved will not miss this opportunity.

PART II

WE OFFER A CHANCE FOR GROWTH:
ISRAELI AGRICULTURE AS A GROWTH
MODEL FOR THE REGION

4

ISRAELI RANGELANDS AND THE MIDDLE EAST

CYRUS M. McKELL

INTRODUCTION

Rangelands are an important asset to Israel's citizens for the many services and products that rangelands provide. Yet the returns from these noncropped, hillside, valley, and desert lands are often overlooked in assessing national strengths and the future. Not only do rangelands provide grazing for livestock, but also runoff water for agriculture, forest, and plant products; wildlife habitat; and natural beauty for lifting the human spirit.

Rangelands, the people who use the land, and those who research better ways to use the land and its products also represent an important linkage to other countries in the Near East, where rangelands constitute a major portion of the land area and management problems exist.

The objectives of this chapter are to provide an overall view of Israel's rangelands and their relevance not only to Israel and neighboring countries but also to countries with Mediterranean-type climates, to describe some of the research under way, and to suggest some ways to improve linkages to other countries. Israeli rangelands have much to offer the Near East by way of technical examples and economic interchange. In a broader context, Israeli rangelands are important to the United States and the world as well if such an exchange improves political and social stability.

ISRAELI RANGELANDS

Geographic Setting

Israel's communities are literally surrounded by rangelands, less so for communities in the agricultural valleys, but almost completely for those in the hills and semidesert areas. Shrub rangelands constitute 40 percent of the land area in northern and central Israel (Naveh 1972). In the southern semidesert and desert areas, the proportion of area used as rangeland increases to 80-90 percent. To avoid a distinction between areas of grassland and shrub land, all should be considered rangeland.

Under the impact of intense use for grazing over centuries, Israel's rangelands have degraded or evolved to plant communities that are composed of shrubs resistant to grazing and to grasses and herbs (Naveh 1967) that can tolerate grazing and yet reproduce to maintain their populations. Often these grasses and herbs are annually self-reproducing.

Climatic Relationships

Israel's location along the eastern Mediterranean coast provides for a relatively favorable climatic regime. As is typical of the mediterranean climate, precipitation occurs mostly in the fall, winter, and spring months, when temperatures are cool and evaporation rates are low. A high degree of precipitation effectiveness is thus possible because rain can percolate into the soil and not be lost in the air by evaporation.

In the southern Negev near Eilat, less than 25 millimeters is the yearly average. Beersheba receives between 150 and 200 millimeters; Tel Aviv and most of the coastal plain receive around 400 millimeters; and only in the Judean highlands, Mount Carmel, and Upper Galilee does precipitation exceed 600 millimeters annually (Atlas of Israel 1956). Four major climatic regions are extant, according to the Köppen classification (Figure 4.1). The long, dry summers exert a strong influence on the type and productivity of Israeli rangeland vegetation. Further, the occasional failure of the winter low-barometric-pressure air mass to develop or remain over the island of Cyprus reduces the amount of rainfall that occurs over Israeli rangelands, thus accentuating the duration of normal summer drought.

Vegetation

Walter (1968) described the vegetation of the Mediterranean region as duriligneous (a shrub-dominated plant community comprised of numerous variants of degradation and regeneration types). Present vegetation is the result of periods of intense use and degradation. In northern Israel, uplands too steep or rocky for cultivation support a

FIGURE 4.1

Climatic Regions of Israel according to Köppen's Classification

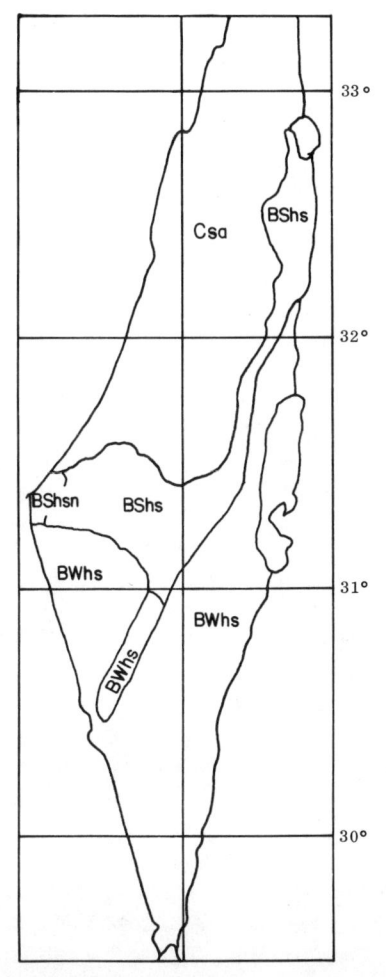

Note: B = dry climate; C = warm temperature climate, mean temperature of coldest month between -3° and +18° C; BS = steppe climate; BW = desert climate; a = mean temperature of warmest month over 22° C; b = mean temperature of warmest month under 22° C, with means of at least four months over 10° C; h = dry and hot, mean annual temperature over 18° C; k = dry and cold, mean annual temperature under 18° C, mean temperature of warmest month over 18° C; n = high humidity, mean summer temperature between 24° and 28° C; s = dry season in summer.

Source: Modified from Atlas of Israel, 1956.

rather dense shrub-land cover dominated by oak (Quercus calliprinos), pistachio (Pistacia lentiscus), and other shrubs with a rich understory of drought-resistant grasses and forbs. Valleys or small areas with soils deep enough for cultivation have been converted from natural vegetation to agricultural crops. Noncropland areas of central Israel south to the margin of the Negev support a vegetal cover of low shrubs and annual grasses, forbs, and legumes. Arid desert areas support a sparse vegetal cover of dwarf shrubs (especially bean caper [Zygophyllum dumosum]), annual forbs and grasses, and occasional colonies of feather grass (Stipa tortilis) in lowlands. Shallow soils covered by a desert pavement, or hamada (Arabic, meaning the unfruitful), and naked sandstone hills provide the main surface feature of desert areas (Evenari, Shannon, and Tadmor 1971).

Rangelands in Relation to Cropland

The relationship between rangeland and cropland use for grazing is one of mutual benefit. Crop residues are used by livestock for feed, with the extra benefit of the manure on the cropland. The residual feed from crops is valuable to the livestock producer because it becomes available at the end of the forage season when forage is in short supply—especially green feed. One of the most commonly available feed residues is the stubble from cereal grainfields. These patterns of land and crop use are traditional and have their origins in antiquity. Increased pressures for bringing more land under intensive production must be tempered with the practical constraint of water availability. The water issue is not one of serious proportions for rangeland use because only a relatively small amount is necessary to provide livestock drinking water. However, other uses of rangeland are restricted by lack of water.

Much of the direct use of rangelands for grazing is by herding of flocks of sheep and goats from adjacent settlements. In the more arid regions, such as the margin of the Negev, nomadic family units graze their sheep, goats, and camels. Thus, the pattern of use and the way in which rangelands serve communities and nomadic peoples is a common linkage throughout the Near East.

Products from Range

The common concept is that rangelands are limited to use only for livestock grazing. However, to the production of milk, meat, hides, and fertilizer from sheep, goats, camels, and cattle must be added runoff water and plant products used for fuel. Rangelands also serve a valuable aesthetic role as open space for communities and a place for people to get away from close contact with each other. From a military point of view, the space provided by rangelands is extremely important for the separation of opposing forces and as a place to maneuver.

Some Problems of Rangeland

Many problems associated with Israeli rangelands are shared by other countries of the Near East, and some are perhaps more acute in neighboring countries. Some of the most serious problems were described by Naveh (1972) as urban sprawl and despoliation, agricultural pressure from a growing population, and overstocking of cattle and milk-sheep herds around Jewish settlements or overstocking of goat and cattle herds around Arab villages. Population pressure on rangelands is expressed in many ways, but two of the most devastating are patch cultivation on nonterraced lands and root grubbing of shrubs.

These problems translate into challenges for the research staff of various institutions. Restoration of productivity, halting of soil erosion, and development of new plant species and appropriate management strategies to optimize their use are some of the problems that must be solved in order to make better use of Israeli rangelands.

ISRAELI RANGE RESEARCH

Early in the history of modern Israel, agricultural research and development was given a high priority. Scientific talent has been developed from within Israel and attracted from without to form institutes and research groups that have gained international distinction. Scientific ties to scientists worldwide make information available from a wide range of disciplines.

Two main research groups are working on rangeland problems. Those at educational institutions, such as Jerusalem University and the Technion (Israel Institute of Technology), investigate problems of a more basic nature, whereas the National Agricultural Research Organization Priel, with its various institutes and field stations, seeks to develop fundamental information linked to various options for improving production and agricultural efficiency.

Research on rangeland problems seeks to reverse trends of previous and present overuse, to increase productivity, to explore new plant materials and management practices, and to develop new plant products. Information is disseminated worldwide in scholarly journals, but direct extension contact with neighboring countries has not been an objective.

Range Research Locations

Within the Ministry of Agriculture's Agricultural Research Organization, several groups are involved in rangeland research. Nine scientists comprise the Division of Forage Crops and Range Management within the Institute of Field and Garden Crops at the Volcani Center, Bet Dagan. Field stations and cooperating staff available to this group are located at Newe Ya'ar in the western Jezreel Valley east of Haifa, the Gilat regional experiment station in the northern Negev, and the Migda dry-land experiment farm also in the northern Negev.

Within the universities, rangeland-related research also receives a substantial emphasis. At the Technion in Haifa, land reclamation and ecology of rangeland management are part of the agricultural engineering program. At Jerusalem University, studies in botany include work on plant adaptation, ecology, and ethnobotany. At Ben Gurion University of the Negev, Beersheba, new plants for use in arid lands receive a special emphasis. Supplemental to work at these established locations, numerous test plots and plantings are located throughout the country.

Nature of Principal Research

Rather than describe in detail the extent of ongoing rangeland research, some of the problems being studied that have relevance to the Near East as well as Israel will be highlighted below.

New and improved plants for livestock forage are a major focus of rangeland research in Israel as well as many other countries. High-producing forage legumes are being developed to provide protein-rich forage as well as to increase soil nitrogen through the process of symbiotic fixation of nitrogen by rhizobium bacteria. S. J. Ellern at the Volcani Center has recently taken on the responsibilities for forage-legume improvement. He is concentrating on selection of legumes that are superior in growth form, have increased seasonal longevity, and maintain reproductive vigor.

Because of the importance of perennial and annual grasses that can produce palatable and nutritious forage under stress conditions and intense grazing management, much attention is given to their genetic improvement and management. Shrubs for use as livestock fodder receive little research attention throughout the world, yet they are a major component of the rangeland vegetation and serve as alternate feed in periods of drought. Israeli scientists are leaders in testing shrubs for adaptation (Koller, Tadmor, and Hillel 1958), response to grazing (Forti 1970), and animal palatability.

Animal-management studies are a standard item on rangeland research lists. However, there is a need for innovative management systems that extend the grazing period, improve uniformity of species selection, and increase animal performance. Sheep-grazing trials at the Migda station indicate that legume-dominated annual forage can literally be grazed into the ground and still return to productivity the following year. Intense grazing on 15 species of shrubs, including Australian saltbush (Atriplex nummularia) indicates that some shrubs hold great promise for providing a good source of high-protein feed and are capable of sustaining a high degree of grazing use in dry seasons (Forti 1971). Other animal-management studies are designed to integrate crop rotation schemes with grazing (Priel 1977).

New Plant Products

Work in the past 10 to 15 years in Israel, the United States, Australia, and other countries on new plant products from arid-land plants has stimulated the imagination and interest of rangeland and agronomic scientists worldwide. Some of the plant species and their products being considered include guayule (Parthenium argentatum), useful as a source of natural rubber; jojoba (Simmondsia chinensis), a source of a high-termperature-resistant liquid wax and industrial oil (Forti 1972); and many species of large shrubs useful for energy, either from direct burning or from some type of biological decomposition. The high cost of energy may generally be considered the main reason why many new species of arid-land plants are considered favorable for production as alternate crops.

Land reclamation tests by staff of the Technion and the Ben Gurion University of the Negev have involved testing ground-cover shrubs, grasses, and forbs for a quick and effective soil cover to reduce erosion and cover the soil surface while at the same time providing an aesthetically pleasing ground cover.

As seen in the brief discussion above, several plant materials and new information on methods of management and use are available from the work of Israeli research institutions and scientists. Most plant materials could be considered suitable for use in other Near Eastern countries.

RELEVANCE OF ISRAELI RANGELAND RESEARCH TO COUNTRIES OF THE NEAR EAST

Similarities among Near Eastern countries are most common with regard to rangelands. All have limited precipitation typical of a Mediterranean climate grading into dry desert climates. Soil types range from shallow sandy loams to heavy clay loam. The most common soils, however, have sand as a dominant feature. Landforms are varied throughout the region, but deserts and uplands are the most common topographic type. Overgrazing and cutting of trees and shrubs are common forms of land abuse. Historically, livestock grazing has been intense from several types of animals, each with different grazing preferences.

Rangelands are important as a social and economic linkage among Near Eastern countries. There is a common heritage of social development centering on the grazing of flocks and the tilling of small parcels of arable lands. Thus, peoples of the Near East share some of the same problems resulting from rangeland use: urban encroachment, soil erosion, disruption of the traditional use patterns between livestock grazing and adjacent croplands, and even desertification.

A few examples of rangeland problems from several of the Near Eastern countries will illustrate the need for cooperation in applying research results and following recommended practices for solving problems.

Syria

Draz (1974) described the deteriorated condition and reduced livestock production of rangelands in his report to the government of the Syrian Arab Republic. Rangeland depletion was attributed to disruptive man-related activities such as cutting of trees for construction, grubbing of shrubs for fuel, overgrazing in the near vicinity of communities, and disruption of traditional Bedouin grazing practices, including lost opportunities for sheep grazing on crop residues of adjacent agricultural lands. Abrogation by recent governments of previous grazing rights without a practical substitute system resulted in free, uncontrolled grazing, which further exacerbated rangeland destruction.

In his 1974 report, Draz outlined a program to control rangeland deterioration. Measures to increase forage availability included the introduction of forage legumes in rotation with wheat, the provision of emergency feed reserves from feed-supplement warehouses, and the planting of fodder shrubs such as Atriplex nummularia. A plan to return to traditional land-use allocation involved organizing the Bedouins and their sheep into control groups to graze assigned areas. A restriction on plowing small areas just marginally suited for crops was recommended. Establishment of sheep-fattening units that would increase the number of animals going to market was given a high priority. In addition, a range-improvement research program was recommended that would cooperate with the Regional Arab League Arid Zone Dryland Research Center in Damascus.

In a brief review of Syrian rangeland problems, McKell (1978) made several recommendations regarding ways to improve the survival of fodder shrub plantings on Syrian rangelands. Subsequent reflections on the general approaches to rangeland improvement in Syria are that great benefits could accrue by referring to the results of work under way or completed in Israel.

Saudi Arabia

Over 58 percent of the Arabian peninsula is occupied by Saudi Arabia, 99 percent of which receives less than 100 millimeters of rain annually. In such a dry region, rangeland uses constitute practically all of the agricultural activity. Pabot (1967) stated that most regions of the Near East whose climates are marked by a long period of summer drought are characterized by overgrazing of all natural vegetation, deforestation and uprooting of all combustible species, uncontrolled extension of dry farming into rangelands, seasonal starvation of animals, erosion of soils, and the extension of desert. Draz (1977) suggested several ways that good range management could serve to combat desertification. His suggestions for the Arabian peninsula were based on several years of experience in Saudi Arabia and in Syria. One of the most important recommendations was to revive the hema, or traditional method of grazing management, which would restore grazing rights to nomadic tribes along with the responsibility to appropriately control grazing. Other measures requiring inputs of funds for research-and-development plantings are being implemented. Critical to the improvement of rangeland is the availability of appropriate information. According to Heady (1973), experts from higher rainfall or cooler areas than those of the Near East have not provided information effective in improving the situation. Sources of technical help indigenous to the Near East, such as Israel, could be of great value if politically allowed to be available.

Iran

Approximately 82 percent of this country is arid and semiarid rangeland. Traditional use of rangelands by nearby villagers and seminomadic operators resulted in depletion of rangelands. Although political conditions have changed drastically in Iran since 1978, the basic conditions of rangelands remain much the same, with most development programs initiated earlier being abandoned. According to a Food and Agriculture Organization (FAO) report prepared by Boykin (1972), livestock numbers were greater than rangeland carrying capacity. Planting of cereal crops on small areas of good rangeland eliminated the potential forage from livestock use. There was a basic imbalance in the forage available from summer, spring-autumn, and winter ranges.

Several years prior to the revolution and the fall of the shah's government, rangelands were brought under national control and management. Grazing areas were assigned to livestock operators, and a number of range-improvement practices were initiated. Some of the more successful practices were seeding of improved forage grass and shrub species, deferment of heavily grazed range areas, and reduced stocking of overused areas. Much had been learned by Iranian livestock operators and professional range managers from studies; from experiences within the country; and from consultants from other countries such as the western United States, where climatic conditions are relatively similar. It appears from reports of former students that the lessons learned have been forgotten, and programs for improving the land and the lives of people using it have been abandoned.

Egypt

Outside of the Nile Valley, most of the land area of Egypt is rainless, except a narrow band of rainfed agricultural and grazing land along the Mediterranean coast. The desert lands support little, if any, vegetal cover of forage value. Even goats and camels must receive supplemental feed to survive if they are left to graze in non-- cropped areas. Numerous schemes for bringing new lands under development have been proposed and are being implemented (Egyptian-U.S. Agricultural Sector Assessment Team 1976). Major problems associated with the so-called new lands are inadequate drainage, poor soil quality, landownership, and development of effective facilities and social intrastructure.

A concept currently being considered for study and funding is the development of new crop plants for arid lands. Such lands, not already under development along the Nile Valley, have been targeted in the Sinai, the coastal strip, and the New Valley (composed of a series of depressions roughly parallel to the Nile Valley but 250 kilometers to the west). Some of the new crop species proposed for the project include jojoba, for its liquid wax; guayule, for its potential rubber; winged bean (Psophocarpus tetragonolobus), an edible bean; and fodder shrubs.

One of the requirements specified for selection of a U.S. National Academy of Science advisory panel for the new-crops-for-arid-lands project was that candidates have international experience in arid-lands development that included Israel.*

The "desertization" problem is especially of concern in Egypt because the threat of sand encroachment on settlements in the Nile Valley and the coastal strip is serious (Kassas 1969). LeHouerou (1968) attributed the initiation of desertization to overgrazing, cereal cultivation, the cutting of woody species, and mismanagement of natural vegetation.

In Egypt as well as in other Near Eastern and North African countries, the desertification problem is of universal concern and common origin. Much could be accomplished by a pooling of expertise, experience, and improved plant materials.

An international program was proposed to the FAO in 1975 by rangeland management specialists for the Ecological Management of Arid and Semi-Arid Rangeland in Africa and the Near East (EMASAR). This program was enthusiastically supported at an organizing conference at the FAO in Rome, but subsequent problems of support and implementation gradually dimmed the hopes of those who conceived the idea. Notably lacking in attendance at the organizing conference was any representation from Israel.

PROBLEMS IN BUILDING LINKAGES BETWEEN ISRAEL AND OTHER COUNTRIES OF THE NEAR EAST

Israel's neighboring countries are aware of rangeland information and plant materials being developed in the various research institutes and universities. This awareness comes either by reading international journals or from contacts with non-Arab scientists who have visited Israel—or who have had Israeli visitors to their countries. Direct and official contacts have not been possible. Even the FAO has found difficult the convening of groups that might include an Israeli representative. The FAO plan for implementing the EMASAR program involved staff contacts with representatives of individual countries and groups to exchange information and obtain help in initiating range improvement and management programs. One key to success that escaped the EMASAR program staff was a dearth of trained people and

---

*The author was chairman of the panel and, indeed, he has had experience in Israel as well as in many other arid and semiarid lands.

a willingness to communicate. Sadly enough, Israel has abundant talent in rangeland research with extensive international experience, but the opportunity to communicate with Arab countries is minimal.

Plant materials being developed in Israel, such as fodder shrubs, forage legumes, new plant products, and even shrubs for biomass, would find ready acceptance and suitable habitats within their range of adaptation in neighboring countries of the Near East.

SOME SUGGESTIONS FOR BUILDING LINKAGES

Scientific linkages to neighboring countries of the Near East and many other countries where rangelands are a dominant factor in the land-use activity and economic structure need to be given greater attention. Through these linkages, greater understanding and cooperation could develop that would improve social and political relations. Four suggestions for building scientific linkages may be worthy of consideration:

1. Use third-party contact to build relationships. These can be initiated at international conferences developed through service on committees of widely distributed scientific journals and organizations and in personal contacts and written exchange with friendly countries where Arab nationals may also be present.

2. Continue to support the international exchange of scientific rangeland personnel for study leaves and short duration, fact-finding observations.

3. Seek involvement in development of projects that have wide international application. Rangeland improvements, new plant products, and antidesertification studies are all of interest to developing countries all over the world. Involvement in such groups will allow contacts and information exchange between countries where direct contact would otherwise be out of the question.

4. Avoid delay in seeking to improve the linkages described above. Israel's advantage as a leader in scientific research in agriculture and all of its applications in such areas as rangeland management is rapidly being eroded by the enormous sums being spent on research at such institutions as the Kuwait Agricultural Research Institute and other centers receiving funding from petroleum sales.

SUMMARY

Israeli rangelands are an important component of the country's heritage, land base, economy, and community development and are similar in many respects to neighboring countries of the Near East and elsewhere.

Israeli range research is vital to increasing the productivity and usefulness of marginal lands, both in Israel and in rangelands worldwide.

Israeli rangelands and their research are highly relevant to neighboring countries. Principal practices and plant materials have great acceptance in neighboring countries.

Rangeland-research results can be used as a linkage to other countries to improve understanding.

Strategies for building linkages are available but tenuous and need to be amplified.

REFERENCES

Department of Surveys, Ministry of Labour, and Bialik Institute. 1956. Atlas of Israel. Jerusalem: Jewish Agency.

Draz, O. 1977. Role of Range Management in the Campaign against Desertification: The Syrian Experience as an Applicable Example for the Arabian Peninsula. UNCOD/MISC/13.

_____. 1974. Range Management and Fodder Development Report to the Government of the Syrian Arab Republic. Food and Agriculture Organization Report no. TA 3292.

Egyptian-U.S. Agricultural Sector Assessment Team. 1976. Egypt: Major Constraints to Increasing Agricultural Productivity. Foreign Agricultural Economic Report no. 120.

Evenari, M., Leslie Shannon, and Nephtali Tadmor. 1971. The Negev: The Challenge of a Desert. Cambridge, Mass.: Harvard University Press.

Food and Agriculture Organization. 1975. The Ecological Management of Arid and Semi-arid Rangelands in Africa and the Near East. FAO Report no. 94.

Forti, M. 1972. "Simmondsia Research in Israel." In Jojoba and Its Uses, edited by E. F. Haase and W. G. McGinnie, pp. 13-26. Tucson: University of Arizona, Office of Arid Lands Studies.

_____. 1971. Introduction of Fodder Shrubs and Their Evaluation for Use in Semi-arid Areas of the North-Western Negev. Special report of the Negev Institute for Arid Zone Research, Beersheba, Israel.

_____. 1970. Grazing Trials on Perennial Fodder Shrubs. Preliminary report of the Negev Institute for Arid Zone Research, Beersheba, Israel.

Kassas, M. 1969. "Desertification versus Potential for Recovery in Circum-Saharan Territories." Paper presented at the International Conference on Arid Lands in a Changing World at the University of Arizona, Tucson, 1969.

Koller, D., N. H. Tadmor, and D. Hillel. 1958. Experiments in the Propagation of Atriplex halimus L. for Desert Pasture and Soil Conservation. KTAVIM, Records of the Agriculture Research Station 9(1-2)83-106.

McKell, C. M. 1979. Utilization of Fodder Shrubs in an Integrated Programme of Rangeland Livestock Production in Syria. Brief report to the United Nations Development Project/Food and Agriculture Organization/Syria Project 68-001.

Naveh, Z. 1972. "The Role of Shrubs and Shrub Ecosystems in Present and Future Mediterranean Land Use." In Wildland Shrubs—Their Biology and Utilization, edited by C. M. McKell, J. P. Blaisdell, and J. R. Goodin. U.S. Department of Agriculture, Foreign Service General Technical Report INT-1.

_____. 1967. "Mediterranean Ecosystems and Vegetation Types in California and Israel." Ecology 48: 445-59.

Pabot, H. 1962. "Méthodes d'étude de la couverture vegetale applicables dans les pays du Proche et du Moyen-Orient." Typescript from author, 21 pp.

Priel, V. R. 1977. Research and Allied Activities. Bet Dagan, Israel: Ministry of Agriculture, Division of Science Publications, Agricultural Research Organization.

Walter, H. 1968. Die Vegetation der Erde, I die tropischen und sub tropischen Zonev. Jena: Gustav Fischer.

5

THE IRRIGATION PROBLEM: THE ISRAELI EXPERIENCE

C. DON GUSTAFSON

INTRODUCTION

The first direct contact the author had with Israelis and the state of Israel was with fellow students from Israel studying for degrees at the University of California-Los Angeles (UCLA) in 1948-50. In 1950 I joined the staff of the University of California Agricultural Extension Service in Orange County, California. Contacts with the Israelis were continued through correspondence, written articles, and educational tours and meetings when Israelis visited California for further agricultural training.

As a developing nation, the Israeli Ministry of Agriculture, on behalf of their avocado growers and with a UN Food and Agriculture Organization grant, asked me to spend two months in Israel to evaluate their developing avocado industry in 1966. Impressed with the research being conducted on irrigation, water use, salinity management, and the variety of crops tolerant to saline and alkaline soils, I prepared a sabbatical-leave program on these subjects. The program was accepted by both the University of California and Israel's Volcani Institute of Agricultural Research, the host organization.

The sabbatical leave year 1968/69 was spent at Volcani Institute working with researchers on common problems of irrigation, salinity, avocado rootstocks, and plant propagation. In addition, while traveling to and from Israel, many European, Scandanavian, and Eastern European countries were visited. During this trip, numerous wholesale produce and retail markets were observed. The purpose of these visits was to evaluate fruit condition on the markets after being shipped many miles from Israel, as well as from California. Quality produce on the market is the result of good production methods and handling techniques.

The most important knowledge obtained during this study year was to be introduced to the revolutionary new irrigation method called drip/trickle irrigation. Dan Goldberg and his doctoral student Baruch Gornat spent time in explaining their ten years of drip-irrigation research and in visiting many of their field test plots. On the basis of this work, upon my return to California, I initiated the first drip-irrigation project on a commercial scale on an avocado orchard in San Diego County. In 1971 and 1979 I organized and conducted Avocado and Citrus Growers' study tours to Israel to study their avocado and citrus production and marketing methods. Special emphasis was placed on the Israelis' advancement in irrigation technology.

ISRAEL: AN OVERVIEW

Israel is located at the crossroads between Europe, Asia, and Africa and between two seas—the Mediterranean and the Red Sea. Its location has made the land an objective of imperial conquests throughout history. Having been ruled by ancient Egyptians, Assyrians, Babylonians, Persians, Greeks, Romans, Byzantines, Arabs, Crusaders, Mamelukes, Turks, and British, Israel became an independent state on May 14, 1948. Israel is a small country, geographically speaking. Land area is 20,325 square kilometers (12,195 square miles). From Eilat on the Red Sea in the south to the Lebanon border on the north is about 483 kilometers (300 miles), and from the Mediterranean Sea on the west to the Jordan-Syria border on the east, the distance is about 64 kilometers (40 miles).

Israel is bordered by the countries of Lebanon (north), Syria and Jordan (east), and Egypt (south). The Mediterranean Sea borders the entire state of Israel on the west.

CLIMATE

Israel enjoys a semiarid to subtropical climate. Situated between latitudes 30° and 33°, the mild climate is conducive for year-round production of many agricultural crops and livestock products.

Rainfall occurs during the winter, November to February. The summers are hot and dry. Temperatures vary within the country from the cooler coastal area along the sea to the very hot desert in the east. Temperatures around the Dead Sea, the lowest place on earth at 392 meters (1,286 feet) below sea level, may reach 48°-50° C (120° F and higher).

THE IRRIGATION PROBLEM / 53

Average temperatures experienced in three climate zones are shown in the following:

	Centigrade	Fahrenheit
Jerusalem (850 meters—2,500 feet)		
August	19°-28°	64°-92°
January	5°-12°	41°-54°
Tel Aviv (coastal—sea level)		
August	22°-30°	72°-86°
January	11°-20°	52°-68°
Eilat (desert—Red Sea)		
August	20°-33°	68°-92°
January	11°-23°	52°-73°

Rain comes during the winter months. Rainfall amounts vary with the region. Following are examples of average amounts:

	Millimeters	Inches
Jerusalem (inland mountain)	486	19
Tel Aviv (coastal sea level)	539	21
Eliat (desert)	25	1

Water available through rainfall is about 1.7 billion cubic meters (60 billion cubic feet or 450 billion gallons). This equals the amount of rain falling on cultivated land. Of this amount, 1.2 billion cubic meters (42 billion cubic feet or 315 billion gallons) are available to agriculture.

Strong east winds, called chumsins, are devastating to crops when they occur. The winds blow in from the desert to the east at speeds of up to 150 kilometers per hour (90 miles per hour). Some regions and smaller areas are affected more than others, but most of the country receives the strong winds.

The chumsin is characterized by very dry atmosphere (humidity as low as 2 to 5 percent); excessively high-velocity winds; clear, bright sunlight; and high temperatures of 34°-50° C (90°-122° F). This climatic condition seriously affects crops and livestock. Crops can be destroyed and livestock killed as desiccating winds occur. Soil erosion, excessive loss of moisture through transpiration of plants, mechanical damage to crops, and crop losses result from the winds. The winds usually occur in the fall but can strike anytime. In spring of 1980, April to June, Israel experienced a series of these winds. Heavy damage was done to crops and affected the upcoming crop. For example, the avocado crop, of which 60 percent goes to the European market, was severely reduced; estimates were about a 70 percent loss. The avocado marketing board had to contact other avocado-producing countries to purchase fruit for the European market.

SOILS

Soils of the Mediterranean Sea area are usually calcareous in nature. Calcium carbonate content is high, resulting in a high pH reading. Special irrigation techniques, utilization of alkaline-tolerant plants, and a different fertilizer program must be considered and practiced if commercial crop production is to be obtained. Types of soils found in Israel are coastal sand dunes, loams, clays, clay loams, desert sands, and sandy loams.

WATER

Water in Israel is a very precious and limited commodity. Sources of water for all uses—agriculture, industry, commercial, and residential—come from the following: rainfall, the Sea of Galilee, wells, cloud seeding, recycled sewage water, and desalinated seawater. A dual-purpose nuclear power plant is in operation to desalinate seawater and produce power.

Water conservation and storage was practiced in the area as far back as 2,000 years ago. Israel has continued the conservation program and improved it through development and utilization of advanced irrigation methods and equipment. Presently, 90 percent of all available sweet-water sources have been tapped. The water is strictly controlled by the National Water Commission, headed by the water commissioner. This government agency is responsible for the allocation, distribution, and control of all available water.

All water, from all sources, is placed into an integrated national water system called the National Water Carrier. The carrier begins at the Sea of Galilee, taking water from the sea and pumping it through pipelines to different areas. The water is placed into catch basins and stored underground for repumping when needed. The pipelines mainly transport water to southern Israel, where the rainfall is less and there is a greater need. There are, however, pipelines to the coast directly west of the Sea of Galilee.

Unprecedented water-use efficiencies have been achieved by the Israelis in managing the limited water supply. Research scientists have been challenged by government officials to explore and develop the maximum production of high yields with present water capacity.

THE IRRIGATION PROBLEM / 55

Irrigated farmland increased from 75,000 acres in 1948 to 400,000 acres in 1975. Additional acreage will be added slowly, depending upon water availability. One of the most important developments permitting more acreage to be planted, and for increased yields, is the drip/trickle irrigation system.

AGRICULTURE

Israel's brightest success story is its agricultural development. It produces many crops and has produced enough to supply the domestic market and to establish an outstanding foreign market in Europe.

Crops

Crops grown in Israel include wheat, corn, sorghum, soybeans, cotton, fodder, vegetables of all kinds, flowers, citrus, avocados, potatoes, apples, pears, plums, peaches, apricots, table and wine grapes, bananas, almonds, pecans, sugar beets, olives, strawberries, rice, miscellaneous nuts, cherimoya (Anona), dates, mangoes, nectarines, and pomegranates.

Livestock

Animals and animal products produced are beef cattle, chicken fryers, eggs, turkeys, milk, sheep milk, goat milk, and frozen turkey meat.

In Israel there are 1 million hectares (2.5 million acres) of cultivable land. Of this acreage there are 420,000 hectares (1 million acres) under rainfed production crops, 150,000 hectares (375,000 acres) of natural pasture and forests, and 450,000 hectares (1,125,000 acres) of nonproductive land. There are 50,000 Jewish and Arab farmers growing crops on 420,000 hectares (1 million acres). Irrigated lands total 190,000 hectares (474,000 acres), with 5,000 hectares (12,500 acres) under plastic.

Agricultural production is mainly based upon the social forms of village and rural life, namely, 230 kibbutzim and 350 moshvei ovdim. The kibbutz and the moshav represent modern cooperative and collective forms of integration, enabling producers to make full use of modern technology and to transform scientific findings into yields.

IRRIGATION

Water

Water is the key to Israel's survival. Without water there would be no food to eat nor food to export to obtain revenue with which to build the country. There is a serious water-potential problem within the state of Israel. In 1948 the potential annual capacity of producing water by conventional means was estimated at 3,000 million cubic meters (787.5 billion gallons) a year. In 1978 the potential was only 1,500 million cubic meters (393.7 billion gallons) per year.

Irrigation of most crops is by sprinklers, with an increasing number of agricultural crops being converted to the new type of drip/trickle irrigation. Since drip/trickle irrigation was originated in Israel to irrigate commercial agricultural crops, a description of the system should be included here to show the advancement in water technology reached by Israeli scientists and farmers.

Drip/Trickle Irrigation

What is drip irrigation? Drip irrigation is the frequent, slow application of water to soil through mechanical devices called emitters that are located at selected points along water-delivery lines. (The importance of the words <u>frequent</u> and <u>slow</u> is explained later.) Most emitters are placed on the ground, but they can be buried at shallow depths for protection. Water enters soil from the emitters, and most water movement to wet the soil between emitters occurs by capillarity beneath the soil's surface.

The volume of soil wetted by drip irrigation usually is much less than that wetted by other irrigation methods. It may be only 10 percent of the soil in the root zone for newly planted crops. Researchers and experienced operators found that at least 33 percent of the soil in the root zone under mature crops must be wetted and that crop performance improves as the amount wetted increased to 60 percent or higher. The amount of soil wetted depends on soil characteristics, irrigation operation time, and the number of emitters used. This number ranges from less than one emitter per plant for row crops to eight or more emitters placed in-line or around large trees.

Drip irrigation differs from conventional irrigation methods in many respects: the equipment used and its management with respect to irrigation scheduling and fertilization, the results obtained in terms of water use and plant response, and the effects of water and salt concentration and distribution in the soil.

THE IRRIGATION PROBLEM / 57

How Is It Done?

Drip irrigation is done by a system consisting of emitters, lateral lines, main lines, and a head or control station.

Emitters, which control water flow from lateral lines into the soil, vary in type from porous-wall (line source) units to complicated mechanical or passageway (point source) units. Emitters will decrease the pressure from the inside to the outside of the lateral, thus allowing the water to emerge as drops. This may be done by small holes, larger holes in series, long passageways, vortex chambers, discs, steel balls, manual adjustment, or other mechanical means to reduce water flow into the soil. Some emitters maintain steady flow at different pressures by changing the length or cross section of the passageway. Rate of flow usually is fixed at from 0.5 to 2.0 gallons per hour (gph); 1.0 gph is most common. Some emitters have manually adjusted rates, some are reported to be self-cleaning, and some flush automatically.

Lateral lines are connected to, or are the environment for, emitters and are usually plastic and of small diameter (three-eighths to three-fourths of an inch). These lines may go long distances because flows are low. Lateral lines generally are one per tree row and one for each crop row or pair of rows and should be installed as near level as possible, particularly for systems using pressures of less than 10 pounds per square inch (psi).

Main lines, which are usually plastic and buried, convey water from the head to the lateral lines. Size of main lines depends upon the number of laterals and the flow of water to them.

The head is the control station where water is measured, filtered or screened, treated, and regulated as to pressure and timing of application.

Meters generally measure water onto a field. Some meters automatically turn off when the desired amount of water has been applied.

Filters and screens are used to keep water used for drip irrigation cleaner than drinking water. To accomplish this, various types of sand filters or cartridge filters and screens of 100 to 200 mesh are used individually or in combination. The sand filter usually has manual or automatic back-flushing devices for cleaning. The cartridge filter is changed when dirty, and screens are usually cleaned manually.

Injectors are used to introduce fertilizer, algaecides, and other materials into the lines. These may be piston-type power injectors or the Venturi-type that create a pressure drop across an orifice to suck material for treatment from a tank.

58 / ISRAEL, THE MIDDLE EAST, & U.S. INTERESTS

Pressure regulators regulate pressure in most systems and are usually brass or plastic mechanical devices. Pressures for different emitters vary from 2 or 3 psi to 30 or 40 psi. Emitters operate best at design pressure.

Clocks are special devices geared to provide timed water applications ranging from 5 minutes to 24 hours for any predetermined number of days. The clocks, which are powered by electric lines, batteries, or water, actuate control valves that turn water on and off as needed.

Advantages

Drip irrigation can reduce operating costs, and this has been the main interest in this new method. Drip systems can irrigate crops with significantly less water than is required by other more common irrigation methods. For example, young orchards irrigated by a drip system may require only 50 percent as much water as those under sprinkler or surface irrigation. As orchards mature, water savings from a drip-system operation diminish but still may be important to many growers who need to irrigate more efficiently because of the scarcity and high prices of water.

Labor costs for irrigating also can be cut, since water applied by drip irrigation merely needs to be regulated, not tended. Such regulation is accomplished by labor-saving automatic timing devices.

Because the soil surface is never wetted by irrigation water, weed growth is reduced by drip irrigation. This lowers labor and chemical costs for weed control. Also, because less soil is wetted during irrigation by a drip system, uninterrupted orchard operations are possible. With row crops on beds, for example, the furrows in which farm workers walk remain relatively dry and provide firm footing.

Fertilizers can be injected into drip irrigation water to avoid the labor needed for ground application. Several highly soluble materials are available for this purpose, and new products that widen the choice are being introduced. Greater control over fertilizer placement and timing through drip irrigation may lead to improved fertilization efficiencies.

Because drip rates are slow, main-line and lateral-line sizes can be smaller than those required for sprinkler or surface irrigation.

Finally, frequent irrigations maintain a soil-moisture condition that does not fluctuate between wet and dry extremes and also keep most of the soil well aerated. Less drying down between irrigations keeps salts in soil water more dilute, and this makes possible the use of more saline waters than can be applied with other irrigation methods.

Technology

The Israeli government, in cooperation with private water-equipment manufacturers, has established a Water Appliance Institute. The purpose of this institute is to test all water-applying devices, whether for commercial, industrial, residential, or agricultural use. Local inventors can submit their devices to the institute for testing and evaluation. Foreign water equipment is obtained and put through intensive testing and evaluation.

The most advanced development in water technology as applied to agriculture is the use of modern electronics, computers, and automation. Because of the need for security along the borders, and because many orchards are planted along the borders, there is a great need for remote-control equipment to turn on and off automatically the irrigation systems. Israeli electronics firms have developed sophisticated computerized irrigation-control devices for use in agricultural fields on the hostile borders. These devices have been so successful that the equipment is now being exported to many countries around the world. Irrigation sprinklers, misters, drip/trickle systems, valves, gauges, fertilizer tanks, filter flow valves, and other pieces of equipment used in agriculture are now being distributed worldwide.

The Israelis have developed their country to a very high degree in a short period of time. Agriculture is the prime example of their skill and determination to succeed. In addition, they have exported many pieces of equipment and knowledge for agricultural irrigation to both developed and developing countries around the world. Their expertise is the result of intense study and research.

Education

Research and Extension

Education is given a high priority in Israel. The following are institutions of learning, some of which are recognized worldwide: the Hebrew University of Jerusalem (general education, medicine, and agriculture); Tel Aviv University (general education, medicine); Technion, the Israel Institute of Technology in Haifa (science, engineering, medicine); the Weizman Institute of Science (postgraduate scientific research); and Volcani Institute of Agricultural Research in Bet Dagan.

The Ministry of Agriculture is responsible for the development of agriculture within the country. The following kinds of organizations are included in the ministry: research, extension, marketing and agricultural produce, production and marketing, export, citrus marketing, credit supply for investments, veterinary, and plant protection.

Research and extension are the cornerstones of Israeli agriculture. Without research to learn about crop production, and extension to teach the farmers, agricultural development would be slow. Many agricultural research projects are conducted on all phases of crop production: diseases, pests, varieties, rootstocks, irrigation, and the like. The most important projects are on irrigation technology, and the bulk of the research is conducted by faculty at the Volcani Institute of Agricultural Research, Rehovot; Technion, Haifa; and the Hebrew University in Jerusalem. Farmers' representatives, acting as members of a research advisory committee, participate in the definition of research targets and in partial financing of research trials of special interest to them.

The Extension Service of the Ministry of Agriculture is available to all farmers. There are approximately 650 professionals, all specialized advisers in all phases of agriculture. One-half of the advisers are university graduates and the others are farmers with much experience and practical knowledge.

The task of extension is to guide farmers toward the most profitable phases of agriculture and to advise them on the most efficient management and production methods. Extension work is carried out by district advisers from ten district extension offices. Along with the subject-matter specialists of the departments at the head office, they form national branch teams. The teams meet 8 to 12 times a year, when the members bring themselves up to date through information exchange and study sessions and decide upon farm recommendations.

In working with farmers of the districts, the extension advisers deal only with their specialities. If a situation occurs where they cannot cope, a multidisciplinary team composed of extension specialists and research personnel is formed to work on the problem. An example could be in the growing of hothouse roses. A district team would be organized to study the situation and arrive at a practical solution. The team would consist of extension advisers specializing in rose production, plant protection (entomologists and pathologists), irrigation and fertility, and farm management, together with a rose researcher and an engineer.

New knowledge is developed and disseminated throughout the country by extension advisers and researchers. They have developed a network of field trials and demonstrations in all crop-growing districts. Since most of the agricultural production is on kibbutzim and moshavim, the grower-members participate and cooperate in these field trials and test plots.

Israeli farmer-growers are constantly seeking information on advanced farming methods, techniques, equipment, and materials. They actively participate in many extension activities, including schools at district and national levels; study groups at the village level; and an offering of over 200 courses, ranging from several days to 13 months at a central school, covering all aspects of agriculture from the basic to the practical.

Overseas Travel and Study

The Israeli government realized early that if Israel was to become a strong and self-sufficient nation, the people must be educated. In the early days of the country's development, funds and grants were made available to send promising high school graduates to overseas universities for training in many disciplines and professions. Agricultural training ranked high on the subject-matter priority list. The University of California received many Israeli students to study for a Bachelor of Science degree in various agricultural fields. Many students remained to obtain master's and doctor's degrees. Also, students already possessing a bachelor's degree came to the United States for advanced study and higher degrees.

In addition to the formal training many Israelis completed, there were many opportunities for these people to attend informal training programs such as seminars, meetings, travel tours, and the like. Funds were provided by various government agencies, foreign grants and endowments, UN monies to developing nations, and heavily endowed foundations, such as Ford, Rockefeller, and other unnamed foreign foundations. Taking advantage of these funds and the opportunity to study, Israelis became well educated and quite able to cope with the problems facing a new and developing nation. As late as 1966, UN Food and Agricultural Organization funds were available to Israel to hire agricultural experts to come to Israel and help train their people. In a relatively short period of time, Israel went from a developing nation to a self-sufficient nation. Since 1956 Israel has worked closely with many developing nations on joint projects, conducting training courses in Israel as well as in the interested foreign country. Thousands of experts have worked in friendly countries on bilateral and multilateral programs. The number of foreign trainees participating in Israeli training sessions number over 10,000. Today, Israel exports knowledge through hundreds of scientists working with 100 foreign governments. Not only is information disseminated to foreign countries, but many industrial and commercial firms are exporting equipment of all types, especially irrigation equipment, to countries around the world. Characteristics of the Israeli people, who have done so much to bring such rapid and advanced technology to their country, are high motivation, enthusiasm, a great desire for education and learning, and superior training.

Israel: An Agricultural Model for the Region

If neighboring countries are to develop as Israel has, there must first be a great desire on the part of the people to develop their countries through hard work. The people must want to become educated, and the governments should provide them with every opportunity for that education. The governments must obtain from developed countries the necessary expertise for the proper training of their people.

Food is the most important product a country can produce. Without food the people will perish. Billions of barrels of oil in the ground will be worthless without trained people to extract it, and there would be no people to work the oil fields if there were no food for them to eat.

To produce the quantity of food Israel has been so successful in doing requires mainly water, trained farmers, and scientists to develop higher-producing crops. Water development is of prime importance. Water utilization becomes an important management program because of the shortage of water in the area. It was agricultural technology in its widest sense that exerted the greatest influence on agricultural development in Israel, largely offsetting the problem of water shortage. This technology is a combination of agrotechnology, research, extension services, and mechanization.

The technology of water use is undoubtedly an integral component of any agricultural technology, and it encompasses a broad range of irrigation innovations, such as drip/trickle irrigation, irrigation equipment, the technical adjustment of irrigation systems to a particular crop, and advanced electronic computer-control systems. Water-use productivity grew by 221 percent between 1959 and 1975. This means that the same quantity of water in 1975 produced nearly 2.25 times more agricultural output than it did in 1959. During this same time, production of cotton increased 130 percent; citrus, 320 percent; vegetables, 190 percent; fruits, 45 percent; and potatoes, 50 percent. There is no reason why neighboring countries could not achieve similar results. Again, what is required is a great desire by government leaders and the people to develop agricultural production to a high level, help from outside countries who have highly developed agriculture similar to the local situation, the means to educate promising students at overseas universities having course work and degrees in appropriate studies, and government-provided strong incentives for the return of the students so their newly acquired expertise can be put to use in developing the country's agricultural and water resources.

REFERENCES

Arlosoroff, S. Efficient Use of Water: Policy and Problems. Jerusalem: Israeli Ministry of Agriculture, 1976.

――――. Israel: A Model of Efficient Utilization of a Country's Water Resources. Jerusalem: Israeli Ministry of Agriculture, 1975.

――――. Management and Control of the Irrigation System at the Valley of Jordan, Israel. Jerusalem: Israeli Ministry of Agriculture, 1978.

Boaz, M., and I. Halevy. Trickle Irrigation. Jerusalem: Israeli Ministry of Agriculture.

Goldberg, D., B. Gornat, and D. Rimon. Drip Irrigation. Jerusalem: Israeli Ministry of Agriculture, 1976.

Gustafson, D. Avocado Industry Development in Israel. UN Food and Agriculture Organization, Report no. TA2307, 1967, New York.

Israel Information Centre. Aspects of Israel. Jerusalem: IIC, 1979.

Kantor, M. Water in Israel: Past Achievements and Future Development Paths. Jerusalem: Israeli Ministry of Agriculture, 1973.

Maas, F. D. 1980 Israel Agriculture: A Short Presentation. Jerusalem: Israeli Ministry of Agriculture, 1981.

――――. 1979 Israel Agriculture. Jerusalem: Israeli Ministry of Agriculture, 1980.

Marsh, A. W., R. L. Branson, S. Davis, and D. Gustafson. Drip Irrigation. University of California leaflet no. 2740. Berkeley, 1979.

Pohoryles, S. Agrarian Structure and Rural Development. Jerusalem: Israeli Ministry of Agriculture, 1978.

Roman, L. M. Israel Agriculture, Summer newsletter. Jerusalem: Israeli Ministry of Agriculture, 1979.

――――. A Letter of Introduction to Israel's Agriculture. Jerusalem: Israeli Ministry of Agriculture, 1979.

PART III

THE UNITED STATES AND THE MIDDLE EAST

6

THE PARAMETERS OF U.S. POLICY IN THE PERSIAN GULF AND THE MIDDLE EAST

AMOS PERLMUTTER

The Middle East, particularly the Persian Gulf and the Arabian peninsula, has become the pivotal focus for U.S. foreign policy in the 1980s. The protection of the production, flow, and trafficking of oil from the Persian Gulf has made it imperative that U.S. policy is precise, strong, and clearly focused and that U.S. political perceptions about the area are clearly defined and realistic.

The Reagan administration's diplomacy must be achieved through military as well as political and diplomatic means and in a singular, consistent way. This is something that did not occur under the Carter administration, which failed to articulate a clear policy and to administer its often muddled policies wisely or efficiently.

A new and strong foreign policy—something akin to the peace plan advanced by President Reagan in the aftermath of the expulsion of the Palestine Liberation Organization from Lebanon—must emerge for the Persian Gulf and the Middle East, replacing old and inadequate policies. The Kissinger-Nixon concept of establishing Iran as a surrogate hegemonial power in the Gulf to protect U.S. interests and the Carter reliance on Saudi Arabia and Iraq to perform similar functions both proved to be failures. It is a policy of searching for regional substitutes to perform U.S. functions, and it is a policy that should come to an end. There is no substitute for U.S. power.

For any U.S. policy to be successful, it must first be cognizant of the political realities and capabilities of regimes and states in the Middle East. This means discarding or ignoring the wishful thinking and propaganda of those very regimes and their apologists.

The first political reality to face is that there are only three political systems in the Middle East that can be described as being stable, relatively consistent, and viable: those of Israel, Egypt, and Iran.* By definition, a political system encompasses more than its identity as a regime, political orientation, or ideological persuasion. For a political system to establish its credentials as being viable, self-sustaining, and continuous and consistent, it must be politically institutionalized, structurally complex, coherent, adaptable, and based in historical tradition. Egypt and Persia (Iran) once constituted mighty and powerful empires with long-established, successful political cultures and histories of imperial rule. More important, Egypt has had the longest centralist administration in the area, while Iran's well-established and modern bureaucracy began to be embedded in the time of the shah.

In contrast, all the rest of the Arab states in the region are artificial creations of the Western imperial powers, molded out of the remnants of the old Ottoman Empire. None of them have legitimacy as functioning political entities; none have political continuity, political institutionalization, or stability. Most important, none have cohesive centralist administrative structures.

No amount of political propaganda or public relations efforts will turn Iraq, Syria, Jordan, Saudi Arabia, and the Gulf sheikhdoms into viable, credible, and institutionalized political entities overnight. They are ethnically heterogeneous, politically fragmented, and socially noncohesive states, with resulting short-lived, insecure, praetorian regimes that, along with their social systems, are prey to revolutionary activities and upheaval.

The Arab states of the Gulf, particularly Saudi Arabia and the oil sheikhdoms, are patrimonial and lacking in traditional political systems. Even as they present a modern facade, especially in economic terms, their political systems are premodern and so are their social, bureaucratic, and military structures.

The common test for viability that can be put to these regimes is how they respond under stress, and what has been happening in Syria, Lebanon, Iraq, the two Yemens, and Saudi Arabia (during the abortive Mecca coup of November 1979) for more than three decades is not encouraging and is, in fact, indicative of the fragility of these regimes. The turmoil, turnover, and upheaval in the area; the fratricidal struggles; and the clearly self-interested ambitions of these states are a clear indication of their own political weakness and lack of legitimacy.

Even with states that appear to have some track record of relative longevity, such as Jordan, Morocco, Iraq, and even Saudi Arabia, the track record is one of appearance only. In all of those cases,

---

*Turkey can be said to be a special case. It is the last remnant of the old Ottoman Empire and possesses a modern, centralized administrative structure.

revolutionary and social forces are nibbling away at the weak foundations of the regimes, although it can be said that Jordan's military is a formidable and consistent political force (which is nevertheless not enough to turn Jordan into a viable political entity).

Most Arab regimes do not fit the ordinary definition or category of political states that even Asian and Latin American regimes can be loosely fitted into. The Arab regimes are praetorian, oriented toward the military, and politically volatile. This is true of Iraq, Syria, Jordan, and patrimonial Saudi Arabia and the oil sheikhdoms. While the military and bureaucracy produced the modern system in the West since the 1790s, the regimes and bureaucracies of the Arab world were created by Western powers and were not indigenous creations but forces created by the British, the French, and in part by the old Ottoman Empire. This process has been further carried on by the United States and the USSR since 1945 and continues to a great degree today. It is a process that has ill-suited the Arab regimes and has not treated them kindly. Arab performance against Israeli military forces in four wars (Nasser's ill-fated war against the Yemenis as well as other localized wars) show that Soviet and U.S. military training and technology are not sufficient to overcome the inherent political weaknesses of Arab regimes that result in poor military performances.

What makes Egypt and even Iran so different from the rest of the Arab states is that their military structure and their bureaucracies, while also products of the Ottoman Empire and the West, stretch backward to a tradition of indigenous empire that preserves their political integrity and viability and helps them to survive even such disasters as Khomeini's revolution. The key is that the bureaucracies and political structures of Egypt and Iran have a base in historical tradition and are not artificial creations of the British, French, or Ottoman empires.

Thus, U.S. policy must be based on reality: the reality of power in the area and the reality of a particular regime's capability for sustaining itself. The realities to be faced in the Middle East are threefold: (1) Israel is the most clearly stable, historical, and modern state in the area; (2) Egypt and Iran are a mixture of premodern and modern states in the area, but most important, their bureaucracies and political systems have firm historical roots; and (3) the praetorian states of the Arabian peninsula and the Persian Gulf have no such historical or political legitimacy; their longevity, their viability, and their stability are therefore suspect.

Considering these realities, what should U.S. policy be? Assuming the abandonment of a surrogate kind of policy, in what direction should the United States go? It is pragmatic to say that U.S. military power in the area should be autarkic and independent. In short, there is no substitute for a U.S. military presence in the area.

This U.S. military presence should be composed of naval and/or airborne forces targeted on rescuing and protecting key strategic areas, areas vital to U.S. interests, particularly in the northeastern part of the Persian Gulf. The United States must be ready to undertake internal as well as external intervention in the lower part of the Gulf. Coups, rebellions, and the overthrow of unstable regimes must be planned for and avoided or aborted.

Saudi Arabia is a principal example of U.S. action or U.S. presence as vital and decisive. The Saudi regime, as noted before, is extremely vulnerable to subversion from the inside and outside. In the last decade, there have been three abortive coups in Saudi Arabia. In 1971 there was an attempted air force coup. In November of 1979 there was the aforementioned political-religious-Yemeni-inspired coup in Mecca, and in late October 1980 Kuwait reported an abortive military coup in an army garrison around Riyad, the capital city of Saudi Arabia. In spite of rapid economic development and increasing affluence owing to their oil wealth, the Arab sheikhdoms are nevertheless not ready to react to, prevent, or reform in order to prevent revolution—certainly not any revolution on the order of what happened in Iran.

Iran could very well serve as an example of an area where the United States could have prevented revolution. Although the revolution spread throughout the masses and was widespread and general, the shah, with decisive assurance of support from the United States, might have acted in a way that could have either aborted, prevented, or crushed the revolution.

In Saudi Arabia and the Arabian peninsula, a U.S. presence in the area, in Saudi Arabia directly or in the surrounding area, could help discourage any coups or revolutions in the making. A rapid-deployment force, which is unfortunately still in a skeletal form, could be useful to protect oil-production centers and supply routes from violent or revolutionary destruction or takeover.

The function of the U.S. military presence would not necessarily be to prevent coups, but rather to discourage them by its very existence. The primary U.S. military mission would be to discourage revolutionary actions that would threaten oil supplies. To that end, a strong U.S. naval force would be necessary to serve as a deterrent and to keep open sea routes to and from the Gulf.

Bases, in short, would be a powerful antidote or deterrent to coups or incipient revolutions. They should operate or be located in the Arabian peninsula, but as yet, the Saudi dynasty is still split over the issue of U.S. bases on Saudi soil, although they did accept Stealth planes for protection against Iran. The Iraqi-Iranian war, the outcome of which could seriously threaten Saudi Arabia, and the continued southern threat from the possibility of a combined Yemen onslaught could very well mollify or change the Saudi policy on bases. Barring an actual U.S. presence in Saudi Arabia, the United States could operate from bases in the southeastern Egyptian desert, the Sudan, Kenya, or the Sinai.

Linkage to the Camp David accords is crucial to U.S. strategy in the Middle East. It (Camp David) should serve as the backbone of a three-state alliance tied to a U.S. military presence. The three states are Egypt, Israel, and eventually Jordan, a prospect not as unlikely as it may appear.

Egypt is the most plausible site for U.S. military bases protecting the Gulf. Egypt is the first backup for an umbrella policy in the Middle East. Egypt could be the first protector of the Arabian peninsula—not as another surrogate, but with the backup of a U.S. military presence on Egyptian soil.

In the early stages, Israel should not be directly involved in the U.S. umbrella over the Arabian peninsula. Israel could, however, serve as a forceful check on both Iraq and Syria. If Iraq eventually turns on its current allies in the Gulf, which it most likely will, Israel could check these ambitions by threatening Iraqi military supplies that now go through the Gulf of Aqaba and by deploying forces along the Jordan River, seriously checking any aid to Iraq offered by Jordan's King Hussein. Israel, in short, could act as a surrogate to check Iraq, which will eventually threaten Saudi Arabia and the Gulf sheikhdoms. Syria, the chief Soviet client, could be deterred by Israel and Jordan.

Essentially, U.S. military strategy in its first phase must be established along three concentric circles. At the center are the Camp David accords, with a potential Egyptian-Israeli military alliance, once Palestinian autonomy takes on some form of legal shape. The makings of autonomy are already in place.[1] This alliance must be flanked by an Egyptian-U.S. military entente designed to protect the political integrity of weak regimes in the Arabian peninsula. The capstone of the umbrella is the eventual participation of Jordan. Although Jordan is now ostensibly allied with Iraq, once King Hussein sees the U.S. policy beginning to take shape, he will not want to be left out and, in fact, will see the paramount necessity of taking part. Hussein, in the finest tradition of Arab politics, is a survivor first and an ideologue second; he can be expected to move to the more promising results of the U.S.-Egyptian-Israeli partnership. He has, after all, asked for Israeli and U.S. aid before (and received it) in his struggles against Syria and the Palestine Liberation Organization.

In the northern part of the Gulf, U.S. policy must be to preserve territorial and political integrity and to discourage hegemonial ambitions. Of necessity this means separating emotional issues, such as the hostage crisis, from long-range policies, however politically costly and humanly difficult that might be. Khomeini and the ayatollahs may come and go, but a weak and divided Iran will fall prey to either the USSR or Iraq or both, a result that is intolerable for U.S. interests. To prevent Iran's collapse, the United States must offer limited but effective military support to Iran or promote a UN peacekeeping force along Iran's disputed borders. The United States could install a two-sided policy: (1) shipment of spare parts and military equipment to Iran and forceful pushing for a UN debate on the Iraqi-Iranian war and (2) a call for a peace-keeping force in place. The United Nations has promoted and enforced this kind of policy before, in the aftermath of the Arab-Israeli wars and in Lebanon. The policy is not by any means perfect, but it appears workable and practical, and it is in the best interests of the United States, which should be the first consideration of any U.S. strategy.

What is being suggested here is not a furtherance of the outmoded policy of the United States as world policeman. Rather, the United States should actively protect long-standing and legitimate states (such as Egypt) and ensure a military presence in the Middle East to protect U.S. interests (the production, flow, and shipment of oil from the Arabian peninsula). This necessitates curbing Soviet incursion, discouraging regional hegemonial ambitions, and establishing an umbrella alliance of moderate and friendly states (Egypt, Jordan, and Israel) to prevent the oil-producing states from falling into chaos. None of this can be achieved without the backbone of a real and forceful U.S. military presence.

NOTE

1. See my essay, "The Palestinian Entity between Jordan and Israel," International Security, March 1981.

7

U.S. POLICY IN IRAN AND THE ISLAMIC REVIVAL FOR THE MIDDLE EAST

NIKKI R. KEDDIE

To understand Iranian actions since the revolution of 1979 and to have a better basis for future U.S. relations with Iran and other Middle Eastern countries, Americans need to know more about the causes of the Iranian revolution and the role played by U.S. policy in that revolution. To plan for the future we should know more about what elements in U.S. policy contributed to the buildup of Iran's revolutionary movement and be able to use what may be learned from past and continuing U.S. policies to improve U.S. understanding and actions not only in Iran but elsewhere.

Although some media and press coverage of Iran has added to public understanding, there has been too much stress on simplistic views, particularly the idea that the revolution was caused by a traditionalist reaction against rapid modernization that benefited the rich and the royal family and disrupted the lives of the majority. Shi'ite ideas, like those of other religions, varied greatly with time and circumstance. For example, in 1953 top religious leaders were predominantly anti-Mosaddeq, not antishah, and they were predominantly politically quietist from 1954 through 1962. Finally, such explanations say nothing about the role of U.S. policy in building up the type of Iranian government and economy that led to a revolutionary reaction.

Those now beginning to publish about U.S. responsibility in Iran, in such differing journals as the Washington Quarterly and Foreign Policy and in several soon-to-be-published books, tend to stress only the 1970s (generally 1977-79) and to consider very few individual policies. Depending on the viewpoint of the writer, stress is put either on the 1972 Kissinger-Nixon blank check allowing the shah to buy whatever U.S. nonnuclear arms he wished without the usual review, or on Carter's human rights policy or Brzezinski's obdurate backing of the shah to the point where he apparently vetoed an agreed proposal to send a U.S. envoy to speak to the soon-to-be victorious Khomeini. It is true that each of these individual policies, and several others, contributed something to the Iranian revolution. Although almost nothing was done by us in the human rights sphere in Iran, Carter's announced policy did encourage the liberal opposition and confuse the shah in 1977-78. It is wrong, however, to give overwhelming weight to any of these policies as a key to what went wrong in Iran, nor will an answer be found by combining any small group of individual sins of commission or omission. Rather, it should be recognized that the major premises of U.S. policy in Iran have remained essentially the same for at least 30 years and that the very implementation of these premises helped create a revolutionary situation. Similar premises and their implementation in other parts of the world may do the same. These premises are interrelated, but may be grouped as follows: (1) Iran must continue to supply the Western world with its oil—as an economic proposition this became tied in the 1970s to the U.S. need to improve its balance of payments (partly owing to Organization of Petroleum Exporting Countries [OPEC] price increases) and sell large amounts of goods and services to Iran; (2) the shah's Iran was seen as the chief pillar of stability in the Middle East, guarding against radicalism in Iraq and Afghanistan and among Oman's Dhofar rebels and essentially taking over from the United Kingdom in the Gulf; and (3) Iran was a bastion against Soviet influence coming from its long northern border and a major base for sophisticated U.S. technological surveillance of the Soviet Union. All three of these premises led us to support a powerful, pro-U.S. government in Iran without much concern for its domestic policies, and all three encouraged us to back huge arms sales to Iran for its rapid modernization.

  To elaborate on the three premises, let us suggest, first, that U.S. policy in the Middle East, as numerous instances show, involves close cooperation between the U.S. government and the oil companies, which has also meant, in practice, cooperation with non-U.S. members of the Seven Sisters (the U.S.-dominated traditional oil cartel); these non-U.S. members were Royal Dutch Shell and British Petroleum (formerly the Anglo-Iranian Oil Company [AIOC]). The nationalization of the Anglo-Iranian Oil Company under Mosaddeq in 1951, despite some attempts at mediation under Truman, led quickly to an AIOC boycott, observed by U.S. and other companies, and to a refusal of U.S. loans to Iran. The Western press told its public that Iranian oil was in danger, but in fact the nationalized company was willing to hire back British and other Western technicians and was eager to export oil, which at the time could only have gone to the West as Eastern Europe had a surplus (as is still true, though not overwhelmingly). It was much more the profits of the major oil companies that were endangered than oil to the West, but an apparent threat to Western oil was made a partial justification (along with a fictitious Soviet or communist threat) for U.S. and British secret instigation of the overthrow of a nationalist government that was still popular, despite its economic troubles. This crucial event, which Carter called ancient history, brought the shah to power as an autocrat in 1953. For the next two decades, Iranian oil production was set by a consortium of Western cartel companies, with minor shares for U.S. independents.

The OPEC oil price rise of late 1973, spearheaded by the shah, had as a little-noticed corollary a huge effort backed by U.S. government agencies like the Department of Commerce as well as U.S. private companies to export other products as much as possible to oil-exporting countries. In the case of Iran and many other countries, this was an apparent success: Iran paid two dollars for U.S. products for every dollar spent by the United States in Iran. The effects on Iran were rarely questioned. Arms, including supersophisticated planes and weapons, drained off large quantities of trained personnel and building equipment to house arms and personnel just when these were needed in the civilian economy, while the presence and, from 1964, the diplomatic immunity of military advisers caused growing resentments. The military drain on cement caused long moratoriums on civilian building just when peasants and nomads, modernized out of a rural living, were streaming into cities and needed housing. The clogging of ports was also arms-related. Corrupation, the huge scale of which caused increased Iranian outrage, was furthered by U.S. arms companies and other businesses.

Nonmilitary U.S. sales and propaganda also increased the shah's illusions about rapid modernization. In agriculture, for example, the U.S. companies pushed sales of heavy farm machinery and entire U.S.-style meat and dairy farms and participated in agribusinesses, all projects that turned out to produce badly, to create new ecological problems, and especially to force huge rural-urban migration, creating a body of alienated, impoverished, and disoriented city poor very important in the revolution.

Second, as far as the shah as pillar of stability in the Gulf is concerned, it was this notion that led the United States to sell him any nonnuclear arms he wished, despite practical objections regarding supersophisticated arms sometimes voiced by the Pentagon. Even under Carter, no longer bound by the 1972 Kissinger-Nixon blank check, this policy continued. Some of the negative results of arms sales have been noted, but it should also be stressed that as long as the United States is convinced that it needs local pillars to defend the Gulf in our interests, it is likely to keep these pillars supplied with sophisticated arms with little regard for the internal or possible external consequences. Various "mistakes" in Iran by the United States, such as ending contact with the opposition and leaving that job to SAVAK or failing to report adequately on the economic and political situation and the state of public feeling, were results of a different blank check given the shah. This was a tacit guarantee to support him as long as he appeared to meet our major foreign policy needs—as he did in all the spheres mentioned above: the provision of oil and a market, protection of the region for us, and help against the Soviets.

Third, Iranian help against the Soviets included permission to install sophisticated monitoring equipment near the border and cooperation in other surveillance and intelligence activities. The great majority of Central Intelligence Agency (CIA) effort and money in Iran went into these activities directed at the Soviets, which is one reason the CIA was so badly informed on Iranian internal conditions (having either one or no speakers of Persian in the country just before the revolution). This policy assumed that the Soviets or the Tudeh (Communist) party were a real menace to Iran, and yet, especially after 1947, there was little reason to think so. Mosaddeq used the threat of Tudeh power to try to get money from Eisenhower, but the Tudeh were not in fact strong enough to take power and never tried to do so. The anti-Soviet and anti-Left policy in Iran is partly based on the idea that the Soviet Union and the Left should ideally be kept out of the Middle East altogether. In fact, Middle Eastern countries that have at various times seemed pro-Soviet and taken much Soviet aid or arms have usually ended up quite independent and, even while close to the Soviets, have not done any of the drastic things we seem to fear. On the basis of past historical experiences, it seems imperative to ask the question, Would it not be worth working for a great-powers arms-limitation agreement in the Middle East, rather than rushing arms into countries (including Saudi Arabia, Egypt, and Israel) now that the Iranian pillar is gone? It seems futile to imagine that we can oust Soviet influence from a vital area on its borders, and agreements rather than arms competition might be a way to keep that area from erupting and thus possibly starting World War III. Until now, however, the U.S. approach to the Soviet Union has been militarily competitive and is now becoming even more so, although the initially more difficult path toward agreements should lead to greater security. In general, U.S. economic, strategic, and political interests, whether on oil, exports, guarding the region, or helping us against the Soviets, all made the shah seem like an almost ideal ally and led us to shut our eyes to autocracy, megalomania, torture, and the real economic and social problems of Iran. Our policies clearly strengthened the shah's autocracy and his conviction that he could do whatever he wished.

What lessons may be learned from the points briefly outlined above regarding U.S. relations with Iran and other countries, especially those of the Middle East? With regard to the future of our relations with all countries, we should at a minimum be careful to listen to and take seriously what their people are saying, and not only the rulers or elite. While the view of many Iranians that the shah was a puppet of the United States is clearly exaggerated, it had a basis in the close cooperation of the shah and the United States, despite the widespread evils and unpopularity of royal policy. Our lingering hope that Iran may again become a bulwark against the Soviet Union may be as misguided as many of our past policies. It may not hurt us if the Iranians wish to be independent and nonaligned; it would be worse to have another "friendly" Iranian government, anti-Soviet and supplied by us, that would become the target of another revolution.

Regarding other countries, our leaders seem to have forgotten by now, if they ever learned, the lessons that might reasonably be drawn from the Iranian revolution. At most a few people look around for governments and discontents that look like Iran—the Philippines are a favorite candidate, and possibly an apt one. For a government to be ripe for revolution or extensive opposition, however, it does not have to be a dictatorial one similar to the shah's. In the Middle East, without attempting specific predictions, one may note that a country in deep trouble, partly because of U.S.-supported policies, is Egypt. The late President Anwar Sadat, influenced by Westerners, early in his rule decided to move away from the managed and semi-socialist economy of Nasser into a more free-enterprise economy with an open door in foreign trade. The results have been and continue to be disastrous, even though some Americans deny this. Population growth and the mechanization of agriculture have brought impoverished peasants streaming into overcrowded cities (as in Iran); free enterprise has meant a widened income-distribution gap and a conspicuous class of nouveau rich (as in Iran); and discontented petit bourgeois and student elements are turning to radical, sometimes terrorist, Islamic revival movements (as in Iran). Sadat, like the shah, had a good U.S. press and was generally popular in the United States, especially for his separate peace with Israel. The popularity of this peace in Egypt, however (and many opposed it from the first), was largely due to the Egyptians' desires to cut down on the expenses of arms and wars and to profit from the Sinai and from economic and technical aid from the United States and Israel. To date, the peace has not brought economic improvements, despite slight recent rises in overall gross national product (GNP), nor has it brought the ideological fillip that the promised Palestine settlement might provide. Unless things change radically, it seems safe to predict that discontent will grow and so will the Islamic and other opposition movements, including the type of Islamic movement that claimed responsibility for the killing of President Sadat. In this situation, although the United States has not laden Egypt with arms to the extent that it did Iran (partly because Egypt is too poor to pay), it is still primarily concerned with keeping Egypt as a strengthened military ally that will provide us with bases when we think we need them. Economically, we have thus far encouraged free enterprise and the open door, with little recognition that what is good for the United States may not be good for Egypt.

A rather different example is Saudi Arabia, whose vaunted stability came into question when a politico-messianic movement took over the great mosque at Mecca and was shown to have branches far beyond what were stated either by the Saudi Arabian government or in the U.S. press. Until then, Saudi Arabia had been thought by many to be exempt from fundamentalist threats, being itself founded on fundamentalist ideology. The Saudi Arabian monarch is not much like the shah superficially, and his country is so lightly populated and so rich that he may escape revolution. On the other hand, the massive wealth and corruption of the royal family, the general knowledge that that family and other high Saudi Arabians do not follow in private the strict fundamentalist rules they force on their country, and the discontent of those not adhering to the ruling sect (including about 200,000 Shi'ites) and of many foreign workers and educated Saudis—all might contribute to moves against the regime. Again, U.S. concern with Saudi Arabia is to keep the oil flowing out and U.S. goods flowing in and to provide arms to help build up a new gendarme of the Gulf. The heavy U.S. presence is resented by many. If it be objected that different policies in such countries would constitute internal interference, we must say that our past and present policies clearly involve internal interference. Favoring regimes that follow certain policies with arms, aid, and advisers pushes governments in directions our policy makers like, even if such policies often culminate in the overthrow of these very governments. More direct interference, as with the overthrow of Mosaddeq, has also been tried elsewhere in the Middle East, nearly always with bad results. It is time for us to reconsider policies that often have the opposite of their intended results and are based on dubious premises.

As to the Islamic revival in the Middle East and its relation to U.S. foreign policy: first, it is a mistake to see this revival, whether inside or outside Iran, mainly as a reaction to rapid modernization made possible largely by high oil income. These factors do enter in, but not in the undifferentiated and simplistic manner in which they are often presented. It is more the nature of the modernization process both in oil-exporting countries like Iran and Arabia and in non-exporters like Egypt that is important. These countries in recent years have seen large and mostly uncontrolled imports of Western consumer goods; the building of technical, managerial, and other skilled personnel; the encouragement of large-scale mechanized agriculture (again with Western input); and, equally important, what is widely called cultural colonization—the large-scale import and adoption, particularly by the urban, Westernized, and nontraditional sectors of the population, of Western television, films, clothing styles, and fads. All these phenomena have led to a reaction in the direction of authenticity, which increasingly means a new, utopian version of Islam, by students, intellectuals, and uprooted urban migrants. The new bourgeoisie with Western-style education and jobs have often remained content with Western-style nationalist ideologies, and much of the old Left remains Marxist; but the new discontented groups, resenting the overwhelming Western presence (in part because they were also attracted by it), want an ideology that is indigenous, anti-Western, and capable of meeting a series of deeply felt cultural and social problems, ranging from growing income-distribution gaps to disturbing new relations between the sexes and within the family. Such an ideology is increasingly found in various utopian versions of Islam and has the virtue of not having been tried recently in most countries, while both Western-type liberalism and Western-type autocracy have, to a degree, been tried and found wanting. While the experience of the Iranian Islamic Republic has been far from utopian, many Muslims everywhere continue to blame its failures on the West and continue to believe that Islam, properly interpreted, can solve their problems. If encouragement by the United States and the multinationals of inappropriate technology and economic policies contributes to anti-Westernism, a very different type of economic approach might narrow the ideological gap.

8

ISRAEL'S CONTRIBUTION TO U.S. INTERESTS IN THE MIDDLE EAST

MICHAEL HANDEL

As an informal but loyal ally of the United States, Israel can make, and already has made, a great contribution to U.S. political and military interests in the Middle East. This contribution is based on a few major factors, the first of which is its central geographic location. Israel is an ideal staging base for operations tout l'azimut ("in any necessary direction"); moreover, it can easily be reached by shorter sea-lanes through the Mediterranean (a much shorter supply route than the one around the Cape), it has two modern ports that can handle any loads in a short period of time, and it can offer excellent land connections from the Mediterranean to the Red Sea if and when the Suez Canal should be closed to U.S. shipping.

Israel also has at least six airfields suitable for all types of civilian and military aircraft, including all of the necessary logistical support. It has, for example, demonstrated its capacity to handle efficiently and quickly a massive airlift of military equipment, as it did in October 1973 (Operation Nickel Grass). An important feature of these bases and facilities is that the United States does not have to worry about their defense against external threats, since Israel, unlike most other nations in the region, will take the appropriate measures to protect the bases. For these and other reasons to be mentioned below, the United States can use Israel for the storage of large depots of ammunition, spare parts, and other equipment.

The second basic factor contributing to Israel's reliability as an ally is its political stability—an element that is rare indeed in a region normally suffering from frequent and unexpected changes of regime, coups d'etat, and shifts of allegiance from East to West and back again. (Such shifts have taken place in almost all countries in the region, from Iraq, Libya, Egypt, and Syria to North and South Yemen.)

In Israel, regardless of which party forms, or will form, the coalition government, Israeli support can always be relied upon both for ideological reasons and for lack of an alternative orientation. Yet another important political consideration is that, unlike most other U.S. formal and informal allies in the Middle East, Asia, Africa, or Latin America, Israel is a Western-style democracy—not a self-elected junta, military oligarchy, or unpopular monarchy. This makes it easier for a democracy such as the United States to collaborate in clear conscience with its leaders and renders such collaboration less vulnerable to political attacks from the liberal Left and Center. Most Muslim and Arab countries in the region will no doubt be primarily loyal to Arab and Muslim interests—not to Western interests; their concern for Western causes will be secondary at best.

The third factor is Israel's military strength. Israel's military power and invaluable military experience make it one of the strongest countries in the world today. The Israeli air force is the third largest air force in the world, with excellent pilots and maintenance crews and more than 600 of the most modern fighter and figher-bomber aircraft. It also has close to 3,000 modern tanks, over 5,000 APCs and IFVs, modern and mobile artillery, a highly mobile antitank capacity, and its own advanced military industry.* Israel's military power is not an unknown quantity but has been tested and proved under the most adverse conditions. One great advantage of Israeli power is that it can be mobilized on short notice, because it relies primarily on actual power, whereas the United States relies primarily on potential power, which can take a long time to mobilize. This power can be used not only for self-defense but also for throwing its weight on the regional scales of the balance of power, as has been done in the past. In the event of an exceptional emergency or a world crisis, depending on the circumstances, Israel could be expected to fight beside the United States to protect the interests of the Western world. From this point of view, Israel's military strength may be one of the best long-range security investments the United States has made anywhere in the world since the end of World War II.

---

*In qualitative terms, the Israeli armed forces are comparable to any army in the world. The forces of Iran, Iraq, or Saudi Arabia—even if they appear to possess large quantities of the most modern armaments—cannot be evaluated on a similar basis. A common U.S. error has been (and continues to be) the evaluation of the Iranian or Saudi armies (equipped with the latest U.S. military gadgets) at face value (that is, as if they were equal to U.S. units). As the recent war between Iraq and Iran has shown, these armies may in fact prove to be more of a burden than a help in their own and regional defense, given the poor quality of manpower and maintenance.

82 / ISRAEL, THE MIDDLE EAST, & U.S. INTERESTS

Given the existing U.S.-Israeli tradition of collaboration and the large number of common interests in the region, Israeli-U.S. cooperation would be easy to continue and develop. This could be accomplished (although it need not be) in a discreet, low-profile manner that would not detract from its effectiveness. It therefore does not require any formal or ceremonial agreements but should be based on routine consultations and on an ad hoc mode of action and cooperation.

What are some of the more specific contributions Israel can make to U.S. interests in the region? First, Israel can offer the United States air, sea, and land bases for operation, either on a routine or emergency basis. As mentioned above, such bases are conveniently located for logistical support and are close enough to most areas where U.S. intervention might be required. These bases could be used for direct military, intelligence, electronic warfare, reconnaissance, or any other support operations or as intermediary second-echelon bases for organization, supplies, and maintenance. Israeli bases offer the most modern facilities, and the fact that the Israelis use the same aircraft, tanks, and U.S.-made equipment in general may ease the maintenance burden and the supply of spare parts in an emergency. Most Arab countries, on the other hand, are not very familiar with U.S. equipment; they are familiar with Soviet and European military hardware but find it difficult to operate and maintain without external assistance in any case. In addition, the United States will undoubtedly be able to use Israeli bases for intelligence bases—for reconnaissance, radar stations, ground satellite and communications centers, forward or intermediary command communications, and control systems.

Still another advantage of maintaining bases in Israel would be their low visibility. For the Arab countries, such as Egypt or Saudi Arabia, there are many political and cultural problems that might make the presence of U.S. and Western troops a highly sensitive issue. These countries might nevertheless tacitly welcome the nearby presence of U.S. troops in Israel to protect their interests. Thus, a relatively large U.S. presence in the region need not be provocative and visible, but could still be close to the action when needed.

Second, Israel can make a significant contribution to U.S. interests in the region and to regional stability even in the absence of a direct U.S. presence in local bases. In case of a threat to friendly Arab regimes (such as Jordan, Saudi Arabia, the Persian Gulf states, Lebanon, or even Egypt) from neighboring countries backed by outside powers, a counterthreat of Israeli intervention to maintain the status quo and the equilibrium of the region can be of the greatest importance. For example, Israel's public statements that it would intervene against a Syrian attack on Jordan in 1970 may have saved King Hussein from a Syrian invasion. During this crisis, the Israeli government directly coordinated its actions with the White House and even with King Hussein. Despite the absence of prior planning or early coordination of plans, this ad hoc collaboration was very successful. Similarly, Israel's presence and power may have saved King Hussein from another Syrian attack during the Iraqi-Iranian war in the fall and winter of 1980. (Earlier Israeli cooperation in 1958 allowed U.K. forces from Cyprus to be sent to Amman over Israeli air space to rescue Hussein from a Nasserite coup.)

Third, Israeli military experience can be of great assistance to the U.S. armed forces in a region in which the United States has had little military experience. Israeli intelligence is probably as familiar as that of the United States with the military, political, cultural, and religious affairs of this area. It can also be safely assumed that Israeli covert operations in the Middle East are better cultivated than those of the United States. Moreover, the fact that many Israelis immigrated to Israel from various countries in the region gives them a better knowledge of the languages, mentality, and other factors necessary for a better analysis and interpretation of the information collected in the region. Furthermore, the large number of Israelis of Russian origin can, when necessary, be of the greatest help in real time interception and translation of communications in Russian.

The United States can learn much from Israeli experience in desert warfare and warfare in the climatic conditions of the Middle East. The Israelis have also developed special tactics suitable for desert operations from which the United States could benefit. Certainly in whatever concerns the development of air warfare tactics, particularly air-to-air dogfights and interceptions, as well as tank warfare, there is probably no other nation in the world that has developed and refined such tactics to the level that the Israelis have. In all of these areas, Israel is the only Western country that has recent experience.

The United States can also take advantage of recent Israeli experience in conventional warfare to collaborate in the development of new weapons systems—an area in which the Israelis have a wealth of innovative ideas but inadequate financial support. For example, the Israelis have great experience in, and interesting ideas concerning, the production of modern tanks, APCs, and fighter aircraft; they have developed very advanced weapons systems of their own and have made important suggestions concerning the operation of U.S. aircraft, a platform for the TOW antitank missile system, instant repair of helicopter rotor blades, and numerous other creative weapons systems.

In 1956, 1967, and 1973, the United States obtained much information from the Israelis on Soviet weapons systems captured by the IDF. Many of these weapons were inspected by U.S. experts and some were shipped to the United States (these included Soviet tanks such as the T-62, radar equipment, and antiaircraft missiles). The large inventories of Soviet weapons captured by Israel can also be purchased by the United States and shipped to conflict areas such as Afghanistan to support covert operations. In addition, the United States has also obtained extremely valuable information from the Israelis concerning the performance of U.S. weapons systems—information that has already facilitated the improvement and redesigning of U.S. weapons.

There are also many weapons systems developed and produced by Israel that either do not exist at all in the United States or that are better than similar U.S. designs. These could be purchased or produced by permission in the United States.

Israel has the longest experience in combating international terrorism as well as in developing strategies to deal with terrorism from within. The war against terrorism, which in all probability will become more widespread in the 1980s, requires the development of suitable countermeasures, countertactics, special weapons, and perhaps above all a finely tuned intelligence system. Here again, there is much that the United States could acquire from Israel in all of these dimensions. The area of counterterror operations is certainly of utmost relevance and importance; the unfortunate fate of the U.S. rescue operation in Iran demonstrated how little experience the United States has in this type of operation, which differs considerably from routine military operations.

For its part, the United States has to adopt a constructive policy that would allow it to take the greatest possible advantage of Israeli friendship and support. The friendship fostered by the United States with other nations in the region need not contradict its support of Israel, and it is vital that the United States strengthen (and not undermine, as has sometimes been the case in the past) Israeli military might. Above all, is it imperative from a psychological as well as economic point of view that the United States reduce its dependence on Arab oil; it must also try to separate the oil issue from other regional issues. Despite all of the claims of Arab states to the contrary, the price and supply of oil is not directly linked to the Arab-Israeli conflict or to any other Middle Eastern conflict. By sometimes helping the Arabs to make a connection between the supply of oil and the Arab-Israeli conflict, the United States invites more pressure and weakens its position. A strong Israel supported by the United States is essential for the stability of the region or for quick intervention if and when the oil fields should be threatened from the outside. Israel's power is one of the best guarantees for the protection and continuation of oil supplies in the future.

There is also a negative side. The weaker and more vulnerable Israel is geographically speaking, the more tempted it will be to preempt at the slightest threat in order to avoid the catastrophic results

ISRAEL'S CONTRIBUTION TO U.S. INTERESTS / 85

of a surprise attack; and even a perceived image of a weak Israel will undermine the credibility of its deterrence and invite Arab neighbors to attack. The best way, therefore, to stabilize the Arab-Israeli conflict is to support Israel's deterrent-force posture.

Furthermore, a weak Israel may be tempted to openly adopt a policy of nuclear weapons, which is surely against U.S. interests and could accelerate nuclear proliferation in the Middle East. This, however, also implies a policy of discouraging other countries in the region (such as Iraq, Libya, or Egypt) from developing or otherwise obtaining nuclear weapons.

All of the above arguments do not mean that the United States needs to support Israel without any qualifications or criticism. In a normal and balanced relationship, this should be understood as part of the exchange between two states. Likewise, the Israelis must be aware of the fact that the United States also has other interests in the Middle East, and that in order to obtain influence, it must supply and support other Middle Eastern countries as well. Finally, the United States should be sensitive to Israeli fears and security problems; and in pursuing a friendly policy with neighboring Arab countries, the United States should minimize the danger to Israel whenever possible. An important part of this policy should be, when supplying weapons to Arab nations, to offer Israel additional weapons to counterbalance any danger to its security.

PART IV

THE SOVIET UNION AND THE MIDDLE EAST

9

SOVIET INTERESTS IN THE MIDDLE EAST

ALVIN Z. RUBINSTEIN

INTRODUCTION

The Soviet Union is heir to an impressive imperial tradition. Historically, Russia expanded, subjugating diverse peoples and cultures and incorporating them into its empire, and continually probed its periphery in order to augment its holdings and influence. It is fruitless to attribute diabolical motives to generations of Muscovite rulers. All empires expand for a variety of strategic, economic, political, and ideological reasons. By the eighteenth century, preservation of the empire often dictated absorbing new lands. The impetus was an ever-changing combination of opportunity, ambition, and strategic assertiveness. The process was fitful but relentless, disrupted only by periodic defeats, internal troubles, or great-power opposition.

For almost a generation after the revolution in 1917, a weak Soviet leadership was preoccupied with internal transformation and trauma and threats from stronger adversaries in Europe and the Far East; but when the external environment turned favorable, Moscow once again made known its imperial desires. Thus, on November 25, 1940, Foreign Minister V. M. Molotov, responding to Hitler's offer of a division of the Eurasian land mass, indicated that Moscow was interested in such an arrangement.

> Provided that within the next few months the security of the Soviet Union in the Straits is assured by the conclusion of a mutual assistance pact between the Soviet Union and Bulgaria, which geographically is situated within the security zone of the Black Sea boundaries of the Soviet Union, and by the establishment of a base for land and naval forces of the USSR within range of the Bosphorus

and the Dardenelles by means of a long-term lease. . . .
[and] provided that the area south of Batum and Baku in
the general direction of the Persian Gulf is recognized as
the center of the aspirations of the Soviet Union.[1]

With the advent of the Nazi invasion in June 1941, Soviet leaders had
to sheathe their ambitions and cope with the challenge of survival;
but with victory in 1945 came a return to traditional Russian interests
in the Middle East.

HISTORIC OVERVIEW

World War II, it will be recalled, brought a number of far-reaching changes to the Middle East: the end of the British, French, and Italian empires and the emergence by 1971 of all Arab lands to full independence; the creation of the state of Israel in 1948; the early cyrstallization of intra-Arab rivalries, whose character and alignments were to fluctuate with each successive internal political upheaval and prove antithetical to the chimerical goal of Arab unity; the growing involvement of the United States as a consequence of the cold war that developed in Europe and Asia and that in the Middle East focused initially on Soviet pressure against Turkey and Iran; the Soviet leapfrog in the mid-1950s into the mainstream of Arab world politics; and finally, the coming of age of oil as a strategic resource, readily and abundantly available in the Middle East.

The residual Muscovite ambition to dominate the lands situated along the southern border of the Soviet Union emerged in Stalin's attempt to exact territorial concessions from Turkey and Iran. Thwarted in this by the beginning of direct U.S. military involvement in the Middle East, his only other venture in the region was support for the partition of Palestine and the creation of the state of Israel. Stalin's motivation was political: to weaken the British position in the Middle East. In 1947-48 Moscow still saw the United Kingdom as a rival and a threat, not fully comprehending that its long-term adversary was already incapable of any independent initiatives that could challenge the USSR in the region.

By the mid-1950s, Stalin's successors viewed with alarm the efforts of the United States to establish a network of military alliances with nations located along the southern underbelly of the Soviet Union, thus exposing the USSR to possible penetration by U.S. long-range bombers armed with nuclear weapons. The extension by the Eisenhower administration of the military containment of the Soviet Union to the Middle East, the USSR's back door, heightened Moscow's anxiety and elicited a new diplomatic flexibility.

Soviet aims were unmistakable: to disrupt the system of Western-sponsored military alliances whose purpose was to contain and deter the USSR; to undermine the Western (particularly U.S.) political-military presence in the Middle East; and to introduce a Soviet presence and encourage a pro-Soviet orientation among nationalist, anti-Western movements. In time, as the strategic-political environment in the region changed, quests for military bases, Middle Eastern oil, natural gas, and markets were to be added. The outlines of a broad, regional Soviet strategy for attaining these objectives emerged during the mid-1950s and 1960s: support for those regimes that opposed Western-sponsored military groupings (that is, the Baghdad Pact and its successor, the Central European Nations Treaty Organization [CENTO]); encouragement for regimes that opted for nonalignment politically and the noncapitalist path of development economically; exploitation of the Arab-Israeli dispute, which Moscow found was a convenient handle for turning Arab suspicion into receptivity to closer diplomatic relations; support for the anti-Western regimes in intra-Arab rivalries, thereby aggravating regional disputes; extension of economic and military aid in order to cement closer political ties; and encouragement, where feasible, of communist participation in Arab nationalist movements. By 1955 Moscow had discarded the central assumption of the Stalin period that Arab nationalism was a charade manipulated by the West, and it sought to strengthen the anti-Western (what it called the anti-imperialist) component of Arab nationalism. It also reversed Stalin's threatening approach to Turkey and Iran and embarked on a policy of economic cooperation and political reconciliation.

The changes in Soviet policy preceded a doctrinal revisionism whose impetus came from a more sophisticated appreciation of the Middle East's landscape. Moscow perceived (as Washington did not) the Arab world's deep-rooted aversion to participation in Western-dominated alliance systems and its quest for an independent position in the global struggle between the United States and the Soviet Union, as well as the uneasiness of Turkey and Iran about the U.S. move toward some kind of détente with the USSR in Europe and the Far East.

In 1955 Moscow responded quickly when Egypt's President Nasser broached the matter of arms purchases; and in 1958, two years after Washington had abruptly withdrawn promised financing for the Aswan High Dam out of pique at Nasser's recognition of the People's Republic of China and pressure on Jordan, it agreed to provide the necessary support for the project. With the overthrow on July 14, 1958, of the pro-Western Hashimite monarchy in Iraq, Moscow lost little time in extending assistance for the survival of a new radical, anti-Western regime in this crucial sector of the Middle East. However, lacking the military power to challenge the United States in the area, the Soviet government confined itself to diplomatic backing and shipments of economic and military aid, carefully avoiding any military activities that might provoke a strong U.S. response. Thus, when Nasser flew secretly to Moscow to enlist Soviet support for the Iraqi coup, he was given general assurances and a promise of Soviet military maneuvers in the Caucasus, near the Turkish border, if the Turks moved against the new regime in Iraq; but the Soviets made no firm commitments to act. Soviet diplomats spoke out in the United Nations against the U.S. landing in Lebanon in July and the Turkish pressure, and Khrushchev sent stiff notes to the United States and the United Kingdom; but he flew to Peking to dissuade Mao Tse-tung from precipitating a crisis over the offshore islands because he did not want a confrontation with the United States.

By the early 1960s, the Soviet Union had succeeded in normalizing relations with Turkey and Iran, and extensive economic cooperation was beginning to take hold. The shah's statement in September 1962 that no missiles would be implanted on Iranian territory reassured Moscow and set the stage for close, businesslike relations between the two countries that continued until the overthrow of the Pahlavi dynasty in January 1979.

In the Arab world, Egypt was the prime target of Moscow's courtship. However, with the emergence in Baghdad of the anti-Western government of Abd al-Karim Qasim, the Kremlin began to give it attention comparable to that shown to Cairo. An early falling out between Baghdad and Cairo confronted Moscow with difficult choices: How should it choose between two progressive Arab regimes? How could it promote the interests of local communists without arousing Arab nationalists' suspicions of the USSR?

For a time, Moscow backed Qasim against Nasser, because in contrast to Nasser's repeated expressions of interest in improving relations with the Western countries, Qasim was militantly critical; in contrast to Nasser's crackdown on local communists and assertions that communism was incompatible with Arab nationalism and unity, Qasim brought communists into the government and relied on their support against Nasserite opponents; and in contrast to Nasser's ambitions to unify the Arab world under his leadership, Qasim represented a force for retaining the existing nation-state system, which afforded Moscow more room for diplomatic maneuver and lessened the likelihood of Arab nationalism taking on a bourgeois complexion that might impede the move toward socialism and entrench the position of conservative groups in Arab societies.

Shrewdly, Khrushchev kept Moscow's mini cold war with Cairo over strategy, outlook, and issues from interfering with the expansion of economic ties, as exemplified by the USSR's commitment in October 1958 and January 1960 to help build the Aswan High Dam.

Notwithstanding periodic acrimonious exchanges during the 1959-61 period, Moscow tolerated Nasser's anticommunist outbursts. Moreover, by 1961-62, disenchantment with Qasim had set in because of suppression of Iraqi Communists.

Even more important to the Kremlin, however, was the strategic dimension of its Egyptian policy. Albania's eviction in May 1961 of the Soviets from the naval base they had enjoyed at Valona since 1945, the collapse of the Egyptian-Syrian federation in September 1961, and the imminent U.S. deployment of Polaris submarines in the Mediterranean and Arabian seas prompted reconciliation with Nasser and intensified Soviet efforts to obtain naval facilities in Egyptian ports.[2] This quest for a tangible military presence marked a new stage in Soviet policy in the Middle East. It increasingly absorbed Moscow and led to a muting of political differences with Egypt; and buttressed by the growing interest of Soviet strategic planners in Aden, it was an underlying factor in the significant Soviet subsidy of the Egyptian intervention in the Yemeni civil war after 1962. Ideological and political dilemmas were subordinated to the quest for strategic and military objectives. While aid to Egypt did not bring Moscow a privileged position until after the June war, it did lead Nasser to pursue a policy in Yemen that narrowed his options and increased his dependence on the USSR. In addition, after February 1966, improved Soviet relations with Syria encouraged Moscow to reconcile Damascus and Cairo in order to strengthen this anti-Western Arab phalanx.

ESCALATION OF INVOLVEMENT

Israel's victory over the Egyptian, Jordanian, and Syrian armies in June 1967 had important long-term consequences for Soviet policy and for Arab nationalism, though this was not immediately apparent. Both superpowers had watched from the sidelines as the local actors fought, and even if Moscow had contemplated intervention, the military outcome of the battle was decided too quickly for any intervention to have been effective. In 1967 Moscow lacked, as it no longer did in 1973, a major airlift capability and a Mediterranean fleet that could neutralize the U.S. Sixth Fleet. Its decision to reequip Egyptian and Syrian forces surprised Washington but did not cause immediate alarm. The United States, preoccupied with a searing struggle in Vietnam, was content to let the dust settle. During the next few years, the two superpowers, each for reasons of its own, accorded the Middle East, in general, and the Arab-Israeli conflict, in particular, a low priority. In 1968 the Kremlin was absorbed by the Czechoslovak crisis in Eastern Europe; and in 1969 its China problem took a dangerous turn, as fighting broke out along the Ussuri

River. With the start of the strategic arms limitation talks (SALT) and the coming to office of Willy Brandt in West Germany in the fall of 1969, Moscow, like Washington, had reason to prefer the status quo in the Middle East: Nasser was dependent, the Soviet military had acquired the facilities they coveted in Egypt, and U.S. standing in the Arab world was low.

Prior to the October war of 1973 only one development seriously threatened to set the superpowers on a collision course in the Middle East and disrupt the fabric of Moscow's diplomatic design—the War of Attrition. Originally started by Nasser in September 1968 in an on-again/off-again manner, the Egyptian bombardments along the Suez Canal and occasional commando forays into Israeli-occupied Sinai intensified in the spring of 1969 and by the summer assumed an ominously sustained character. But Nasser's military pressure on Israel backfired and resulted instead in heavy Egyptian losses along the canal from the incessant pounding by the Israeli air force, and by mid January 1970, in Israeli deep-penetration raids that had extended to the outskirts of Cairo itself. Nasser's plight—indeed, his very political future—impelled Moscow to raise the ante sharply, to commit Soviet missile crews, pilots, and air-defense teams for the protection of Egypt's heartland. For the first time in its history, the Soviet Union undertook an open-ended commitment to participate directly in the defense of a noncommunist country.[3] By August Moscow had saved Nasser, stabilizing the situation, and had helped him negotiate a politically face-saving ceasefire agreement. However, the Soviet military involvement caused much uneasiness in Washington, which henceforth gave more weight to the Soviet factor in Middle Eastern affairs.

From the death of Nasser on September 28, 1970, until the outbreak of the Arab-Israeli war on October 6, 1973, the USSR pursued a relatively low-key policy in the Middle East, as it concentrated on stabilizing the détente relationship with the United States. True, on May 27, 1971, the Soviet Union concluded a treaty of friendship and cooperation with Egypt that seemed to entrench the Soviet military-political presence, and in April 1972 signed another with Iraq; but the stunning expulsion of Soviet military personnel from Egypt in July 1972 suggested that a significant Soviet presence did not necessarily signify comparable influence. In retrospect, more indicative of Soviet policy and ambitions was the enormous military buildup of Soviet conventional forces during the period, especially noticeable in the fleet deployed in the Mediterranean and in the continued heavy investment economically and militarily in Arab client states.

CHANGE IN THE BALANCE OF POWER

The October war was a watershed in Soviet policy in the Middle East. It heralded the advent of a new era, in which the USSR was prepared to risk confrontation with the United States in defense of a client threatened with defeat at the hands of a pro-Western regional rival. Dramatically shattered was the bric-a-brac of wishful assumptions collected by the Nixon-Kissinger White House in the course of its search for détente. U.S. leaders were wrong in believing that the improved relations between the United States and the Soviet Union in Europe and in SALT would lead Moscow to curb its challenge to U.S. interests in the Middle East, that the USSR's stake in détente would impel it to prevent Arab clients from starting a war, and that the United States would be able to use the prospect of U.S. economic concessions to obtain Soviet restraint in the volatile Middle East setting. Moscow had never indicated it subscribed to these premises. Its commitment to incrementalism, to a policy of pressing local advantages in the hope of contributing to the erosion of the U.S. position, mocked the ratiocinations of the strategists of deterrence.

In October 1973 both superpowers were for the first time equally involved in a crisis each viewed with the utmost seriousness, not only in regard to their respective client states, but in regard to their relationship with each other. It was the first time they were locked in direct conflict over a Middle Eastern issue, the first time they found themselves in a crisis that was taking place within the broader context of their effort to restructure and stabilize their global relationship in a setting of evolving détente, and their first crisis in a period when the Soviet Union enjoyed both nuclear and conventional military equivalence. Neither was distracted by any pressing problem elsewhere, and oil intruded itself into the consciousness of the decision makers in both countries.

At the end of the October war, Moscow could look back with a sigh of relief and a measure of satisfaction: its Arab clients had scored a political victory of sorts, breaking the stalemate that had prevailed since June 1967 and forcing the United States to pressure Israel and bring it to the conference table. By its lavish supply of arms and readiness to take risks, the Soviet Union had shown itself a determined, reliable patron that had saved the Arabs from another military disaster. Moreover, the Arab oil weapon, at last unsheathed for political leverage, had shaken the Western world, bringing soaring inflation, mass unemployment, and economic troubles. The North Atlantic Treaty Organization (NATO) was in disarray, and the United States was at odds with its closest allies. Yet within a matter of weeks the Soviet success was shown to be as impermanent as the desert dunes.

Hardly had the fighting stopped on the Sinai front on October 25, 1973, than Sadat turned to the United States, sending his acting foreign minister to Washington in preparation for a visit by Secretary of State Henry Kissinger to Cairo, the implementation of the UN ceasefire, and the resumption of diplomatic relations with the United States, which had been broken by Nasser in June 1967. Thus, though the USSR had saved Egypt from another defeat, Sadat plumped Egypt's eggs into Washington's basket, leaving the Soviets on the sidelines, empty-handed and angry. Relations between Cairo and Moscow quickly deteriorated. In March 1976 Sadat unilaterally abrogated the 1971 Soviet-Egyptian friendship treaty, depriving Moscow of all the military privileges for which it had expended so much in the previous decade; and three years later, Sadat signed a peace treaty with Israel, transforming the character of the Arab-Israeli conflict and casting doubt on the Soviet contention that a conflict as extensive and explosive as that between the Arab states and Israel could not be settled without the cooperation of the Soviet Union.

Though obviously dismayed by this dramatic turn of events, the Soviet Union persists and seeks to exploit the "contradictions" that it believes may one day undermine the Egyptian-Israeli treaty and the seeming stability it has brought to this area of the Middle East. It denounces the treaty and the Camp David process that gave birth to it, upholds the Arab rejectionist position, accords new emphasis to its ties with Syria, and ingratiates itself with the melange of extremist anti-Western and moderate pro-Western Arab regimes and movements that seek to isolate Egypt and oppose this aspect of U.S. policy. There is little evidence that the Soviet Union has any genuine interest in a comprehensive settlement of the Arab-Israeli conflict or, indeed, of any of the many regional conflicts in the Middle East, unless Moscow is positioned to assume the role of imperial arbiter. The collapse of its close relationship with Egypt and the reemergence of the United States as a prominent actor in the Arab world were keen disappointments. However, the deposal of the shah in January 1979 significantly altered the Middle Eastern scene and opened new opportunities for Moscow. In the Soviet response to these unanticipated and abrupt turnabouts, one may discern the essential and permanent components of Soviet interests in the Middle East and the underlying considerations that motivate USSR diplomacy.

REALPOLITIK

Soviet interests in the Middle East have undergone striking changes over the past generation or so. Whereas in the late 1940s and 1950s they were primarily defensive, geared to weaken the military belt of interlocking alliances that the United States was creating to complete the encirclement of the Soviet Union, in the 1960s and 1970s they assumed a more ambitious, expansionist approach in response to local conditions and tactical opportunities. The underlying strategic rationale was the projection of Soviet power into all four sectors of the Middle East—that is, the non-Arab Muslim countries situated along the southern border of the Soviet Union, namely, Turkey, Iran, and Afghanistan; the Arab-Israeli sector of the Arab world; the Persian Gulf-Arabian peninsula; and the North African littoral. Soviet interest in each region developed independently, in response to a changing combination of security concerns, military capabilities, local developments, and systemic rivalry with the United States. What is likely in the 1980s is a sustained Soviet effort to pursue a forward policy throughout the entire Middle East.

With experience, Soviet leaders have become more realistic about their prospects in the Middle East and more accepting of the periodic frustrations occasioned by the unpredictability of the strategic environment within which they pursue their imperial ambitions. Gone is the ideological euphoria of the Khrushchev period, when expectations for the spread of communism meshed with Khrushchev's ebullient outlook to generate an entry into the Middle East on a broad front. Doctrine underwent revision, as the Soviet leadership tried ideologically to come to grips with the complexity of noncommunist, bourgeois-nationalist elites nevertheless following anti-Western, anti-imperialist foreign policies and progressive internal reforms, though often with anti-Soviet and anticommunist overtones. "National democracy," "revolutionary democracy," and the noncapitalist path of development entered the Soviet lexicon, and Soviet analysts worked hard to reconcile the advocacy by ruling military elites in the Middle East (and throughout the Third World) of progressive policies that merited Soviet support with their persecution of indigenous communists and readiness to maintain close ties with some Western countries. But after Khrushchev's deposal in October 1964 and the increasingly frequent internal upheavals that ousted the paragons of progressivism in Indonesia, Ghana, Mali, Egypt, and Iraq, Moscow downgraded attempts to devise ideologically consistent typologies for categorizing Third World countries and pushed the building of influence and acquisition of military facilities. For Brezhnev, strategic calculations overshadowed the fixation with ideological coherence, though the quest for the latter continued to absorb the attention of some Soviet academics.

A leading Soviet scholar, G. I. Mirskii, epitomized the retreat from doctrinal preoccupations. In the early 1960s he had, with Khrushchev's backing, been in the forefront of the effort to update and rationalize the Soviet ideological framework for analyzing political and socioeconomic developments in the Third World. In particular, he pioneered the view that the military had to be assessed as a distinct social substratum of society in terms of the actual role that it played in different countries, in some instances being progressive, in others reactionary. In the 1960s, as military coups spread across the Third World, this led to a benevolent assessment of their socioeconomic and political role, which was often seen as anti-imperialist and pro-Soviet. However, by the mid-1970s, Mirskii argued that the military-state-capitalist model, though introducing some reform and weakening the big bourgeoisie, was incapable of transforming society; moreover, in its preoccupation with retaining power, the military caste lost its progressive character and unleashed the very instability it had purportedly sought to overcome. The result was endemic instability and political wavering. This led Mirskii to a pessimistic conclusion that contrasted with his relative optimism in the 1960s.

> Thus, one can draw the conclusion that even if the army in "The Third World" is able to play a progressive, revolutionary role in the stage of struggle for national independence and the liquidation of feudal domination, in the stage of the deepening social revolution there will be manifested a conservative and antidemocratic tendency, which determines its "peculiarities," namely, in the words of F. Engels, its corporateness, its interests. This is exactly what imperialism counts on. To consider the army as the leading force of the anticapitalist revolution and the leader of society in countries with a socialist orientation would be a serious mistake.
> The only condition guaranteeing a genuine democratic, progressive development of the nations of Asia, Africa, and Latin America is the creation of a vanguard party, which has adopted the position of scientific socialism [that is, the position espoused by the communist party of the Soviet Union]. Such a party must assume leadership of the army and promote its transformation into a truly national armed forces, freed from the spirit of "elitism" and exclusiveness. In this respect, the history of the Soviet Army serves as an unsurpassed model, having become under the leadership of the communist party the reliable instrument for the defense of socialist achievements.[4]

Inherent in Mirskii's analysis is not merely disenchantment with the military as a social group capable of promoting communist or pro-Soviet policies, but implicit acknowledgment that for the foreseeable future realpolitik is the really constant calculation determining alignments in the Third World and, presumably, the basis on which Soviet policy should be predicated. Careful examination of the pattern of actual Soviet behavior in the Middle East over the past generation reveals that the Soviet leadership acted on the basis of such an assumption.

One final note on the effort to bring ideology in accord with reality. In the late 1970s some Soviet scholars began reexamining the USSR's economic relationships with the Third World "in the light of new perceptions about the nature of the world economy and the USSR's place in it" and questioning "the traditional Manichaean view of world economics, in which the socialist and capitalist camps compete for the exclusive control of Third World resources."[5] Their arguments that advances in science and technology militate toward global interdependence could, if accepted, bring important changes in the policy pursued by the Soviet government in the Third World. But for the time being, their writings bear little relationship to the actual policies of their government.

SOVIET STRATEGY

A number of generalizations about Soviet policy in the Middle East can be distilled from the record of Soviet behavior.[6] The continuities are striking. First, the Soviet Union has pursued a differentiated policy that has been sensitive to constraints and opportunities. The choice of targets, the proffering of aid packages, the willingness to subordinate Soviet desires to a courted country's preferences, and the businesslike fashion in which most agreements have been carried out, irrespective of occasional policy disputes, bespeak a sound perception of priorities and approach. The USSR has learned to cope with ambiguity and the dilemmas of pursuing conflicting objectives. Thus, Khrushchev managed to accommodate Egypt's Nasser and Iraq's Qasim, despite quarrels over local communists, and to maintain good relations with each, despite their mutual contentiousness. Brezhnev put up with Sadat's querulousness, and when this no longer proved possible he moved on to other prospects. In general, he maneuvered deftly in regional rivalries, managing to sustain good relations with both sides, for example, in the quarrels between Iraq and Iran, Syria and Iraq, the Yemen Arab Republic (YAR) and the People's Democratic Republic of Yemen (PDRY), and Kuwait and Iraq.

Second, strategic considerations, not ideological impulses, guided Soviet diplomacy. Neither the shah's conservatism, Khomeini's Islamic revivalism, Sadat's de-Nasserization, Qaddafi's brand of fundamentalism, nor Turkey's endemic anti-Russianism has deterred Moscow's quest for closer state-to-state relations. In all instances, local communists have been expendable. The strategic interests have been clear: to undermine the U.S. system of military alliances and deprive Washington of military footholds in the region; to acquire military bases that would enable the USSR to collect intelligence, build up stockpiles of arms, and use its forces to affect political outcomes; and to prevent any consolidation of U.S. power in the region. Geostrategically, Moscow appreciates that the prizes are valuable, the stakes relatively small (compared, let us say, with those required in Europe and the Far East), and the outcome of the "great game" very much up for grabs.

Third, the Soviet Union has been a reliable patron-protector. Its readiness to shield prime clients from defeat at the hands of their pro-U.S. rivals has enhanced its overall creditability. At times, this meant that it had to yield to a client's preferences. From 1967 on, there has not been one instance in which Moscow sought to whittle away or renege on a basic commitment. It footed the bill—in 1969-70 during Nasser's War of Attrition along the Suez Canal, in October 1973, in 1974-75 during the Iraqi-Iranian crisis, and in 1976 during Syria's intervention in Lebanon.

A departure from this record may be in the offing. Throughout the Iraqi-Iranian war, which began on September 22, 1980, the USSR has tried to play the role of honest broker, maintaining its commitment minimally to Iraq in line with the 1972 friendship treaty, but trying also to improve relations with Tehran's quasi-anarchic and divided leadership. Though linked by treaty to Iraq, Moscow is inevitably intrigued by the possibility that the larger, more populous, more economically important, and strategically pivotal Iran could well fall into its waiting lap, so it has proceeded cautiously in its quest for leverage over both countries.

Fourth, it is in Moscow's interest to fuel Middle Eastern arms races in all sectors of the region, because it knows that its principal attraction for anti-Western Muslim states (whose internal political orientation is immaterial to Soviet leaders) derives from the ability to supply them with weapons to retain power and to shield them from possible defeat at the hands of a Western-backed rival. Arms do not directly bring influence, but they enable Moscow to strengthen opposition to the United States and its friends in the region. Moscow's arsenal is always ready for business, big and small, whether to provision Syria's military buildup and enable Hafez Assad to tighten his grip on domestic dissidents, sustain his army of occupation in northern Lebanon, and resist U.S. offers to negotiate a settlement with Israel (which would diminish the Kremlin's leverage in the Soviet-Syrian relationship); or whether to funnel arms to the PDRY and intensify the pressure on Saudi Arabia. As the world's largest producer of conventional weapons, Moscow has enormous stockpiles to draw from and uses arms as any would-be benefactor uses alms.

Finally, running through Soviet policy and interest in the Middle East is the central aim of eroding U.S. position and influence. Underlying all that has transpired in the past generation is the Soviet assumption that the United States is the principal adversary. Moscow correctly concludes that Washington's aim is to keep the Soviet Union out of the region. Accordingly, no temporary accommodation or compromise can alter the permanence of their strategic rivalry. Indeed, time and again Moscow has shown by its behavior that the prospect of improved relations with the United States does not, to Washington's continual surprise, take precedence over the USSR's determination to pursue its strategic and political objectives in the Middle East, be they in Afghanistan, Iran, Iraq, the PDRY, Syria, or Libya: the U.S. connection is expendable, the Middle Eastern is not. Derangement of the U.S. position, not rapprochement, is the key to understanding Soviet strategy in the Middle East.

SOVIET FUTURE IN THE MIDDLE EAST

Oil, the fall of the shah, the Soviet invasion of Afghanistan, and the eruption of the Iraqi-Iranian conflict that may well be the Arab-Israeli conflict of the 1980s have all riveted the superpowers' rivalry on the Persian Gulf-Arabian peninsula quadrant of the Middle East. It is here that the superpowers may have to exercise extraordinary prudence in the years ahead to forestall a confrontation that neither seeks. For both Moscow and Washington, the Middle East holds a place of pride in strategic thinking that started in the early 1970s and is certain to continue and intensify in the decades ahead. The indeterminate nature of their rivalry in the Middle East poses a danger to their search for strategic stability. Events, unguided and unanticipated, may impose unwanted designs on their tentative blueprints for cooperation.

Accordingly, it is especially appropriate that attention be directed to the principal changes in Soviet behavior since the October war, which may have profound consequences for the future of the Soviet-U.S. rivalry, not only regionally but globally as well. The most notable change in Soviet behavior has been in Moscow's ability and readiness to project power into areas of opportunity. The Soviet Union is the possessor of an awesome conventional capability that was dramatically displayed in the Arab-Israeli war in October 1973, in Angola in 1975-76, in Ethiopia in 1977-78, and in Afghanistan since December 1979. The massive buildup of Soviet conventional forces, which gained momentum in the late 1960s, shows no signs of abating. The USSR has developed a strategic airlift capability, complete with long-range transports and seven airborne divisions; it has a bluewater fleet consisting of very modern cruisers and helicopter carriers of the Kiev class, and large numbers of support ships; and it has a merchant fleet that includes roll-off, roll-on ships that sharply reduce the time needed to remain in port and high-speed naval hoverwarships.[7] All of this enhances the USSR's ability to undertake forward deployments, in support of clients and in response to political opportunities. This Soviet force projection capability is steadily growing, though it is probably not yet of such a size as successfully to challenge a determined U.S. countercapability in the Persian Gulf or Eastern Mediterranean.

A second important change in Soviet behavior, and one that is directly a function of the previously mentioned development, is the USSR's pursuit of a slightly more venturesome policy than heretofore. Especially prior to the expulsion of the Palestine Liberation Organization from Lebanon, Moscow had been running higher risks for regional gain, accepting the international costs and consequences, and doing so irrespective of the effect on its relationship with the United States. (It may do so because it perceives the United States as weak, internally divided, and lacking the steadiness of outlook necessary for a prolonged imperial rivalry.) The case of Afghanistan is the prime example, but there are others as well. Syria's military intervention in Lebanon is possible in great measure because of a steady stream of weaponry and assurance, sealed in October 1980 by the friendship treaty that Syrian President Assad has assiduously avoided for almost a decade. This and the gathering of USSR weapons for shipment to Cuba, which in turn is apparently smuggling them to guerrillas in El Salvador,[8] illustrate the range of undertakings that Moscow is willing to subsidize as part of its forward policy. In no crisis in the Middle East since 1967 has the Soviet Union deferred to U.S. preferences. Increasingly, Moscow influences the course of regional crises. The Soviet Union's confidence in its military might, its conviction that the correlation of forces favors the Soviet camp, its awareness of U.S. self-doubt and the domestic fetters on Washington's turn to the military option, its determination to play a prominent role in the management of regional conflicts, and its expectation of a ripple effect that will lead more and more Middle Eastern leaders to Moscow to reach an accommodation all undoubtedly strengthen the case of those in the Kremlin who favor greater activism in situations of opportunity.

Finally, militarily and geopolitically, Moscow is today well-positioned to exploit future upheavals and systemic instabilities caused by the lurch of traditionalist Middle Eastern societies toward modernity. In the Middle East, the angry, unhinged mixture of fundamentalists, radicals, Muslim Luddites, and would-be Mahdis seems more likely to sow disunity than unity, internal stagnation and dislocation than a new order based on Koranic principles, vulnerability to outside pressures than genuine independence—and new opportunities for the advance of Soviet imperial ambitions. Through its multitiered network of diplomats, KGB operatives, and local communists, the Soviet Union can promote its strategic objectives in a variety of ways.

After all is said, it is still true that the Soviet Union has yet to acquire direct and firm influence over any country in the Middle East, though Afghanistan is slowly being overwhelmed by force. But it has exploited skillfully regional instabilities and U.S. inconstancy, with the result that in recent decades one can discern a decided improvement in the strategic environment within which Soviet diplomacy seeks to advance the Kremlin's objectives.

Soviet policy has been remarkably free from the vagaries of domestic politics and ideological rigidity; it demonstrates an impressive pragmatism and sense of priorities, interlaced with a keen appreciation of geopolitical realities and regional power balances. Opportunistic to the core, its underlying strategic rationale is to undermine the position of the United States and, wherever possible, to substitute itself as the main power in the area. Ambition, capability, determination, and persistence make the Soviet Union a formidable opponent in the Middle Eastern arena.

NOTES

1. U.S., Department of State, Nazi-Soviet Relations, 1939-41, ed. R. J. Sontag and J. S. Beddie (Washington, D.C.: Government Printing Office, 1948), pp. 258-59.

2. George S. Dragnich, "The Soviet Union's Quest for Access to Naval Facilities in Egypt Prior to the June War of 1967," in Soviet Naval Policy: Objectives and Constraints, ed. Michael McGwire, Ken Booth, and John McDonnell (New York: Praeger, 1975), pp. 252-69.

3. Alvin Z. Rubinstein, Red Star on the Nile: The Soviet-Egyptian Influence Relationship since the June War (Princeton, N.J.: Princeton University Press, 1977), p. 110.

4. G. I. Mirskii, "Tretii mir": obshchestvo, vlast', armiia [The Third World: society, power, army] (Moscow: Nauka, 1976), p. 385.

5. Elizabeth Kridl Valkenier, "The USSR, the Third World, and the Global Economy," Problems of Communism, July-August 1979, p. 17.

6. This section draws on the final part of the author's essay, "The Evolution of Soviet Strategy in the Middle East," Orbis 24, no. 2 (Summer 1980): 332-37.

7. For an assessment of the use of Soviet naval power in the service of the USSR's foreign policy goals, see Bradford Dismukes and James M. McConnell, eds., Soviet Naval Diplomacy (New York:

Pergamon Press, 1979). A broader overview of the Soviet use of military force to promote political objectives is found in Stephen S. Kaplan, *Diplomacy of Power: Soviet Armed Forces as a Political Instrument* (Washington, D.C.: Brookings Institution, 1981).

8. New York *Times*, February 20, 1981.

10

FAITHFUL AGENTS
AND HONEST BROKERS:
EASTERN EUROPEAN POLICIES
IN THE MIDDLE EAST

TROND GILBERG

INTRODUCTION: OPPORTUNITIES AND LIABILITIES

During the 1970s the Eastern European states became more heavily involved in the Middle East than at any time previously. This increased level of activity derived from a number of sources. First, the states of Eastern Europe achieved a measure of autonomy in foreign policy in this period; the Soviet Union was unwilling or unable (or both) to maintain the kind of iron control over the foreign affairs of the so-called bloc that the Kremlin had exercised during the Stalinist era. Furthermore, the Brezhnev approach to foreign policy in fact allocated a certain place for some of the Eastern Europeans as auxiliaries of Soviet policy in selected areas, and this carried with it the need for corresponding room to maneuver on the part of the East Germans, Czechoslovaks, and others.[1]

Second, internal developments in Eastern Europe in the post-Stalinist era had brought to the fore more nationally minded political elites in many of the states, and these leaders were determined to exercise greater initiative in foreign policy, partly as an attempt to bolster their weak positions in the hearts and minds of the local populations over whom they still ruled by means of autocratic methods and poorly functioning economic centralization. The very dynamics of the modernization process and the unfolding political developments of Eastern Europe carried with them the need for a more assertive and semi-independent foreign policy.[2]

Third, and perhaps most important, the energy crisis hit the Council for Mutual Economic Assistance (COMECON) full force after 1973 and necessitated a more active policy by the leaders of Eastern Europe in the Middle East, where the most easily accessible oil reserves outside the bloc itself could be located. This situation was further aggravated by the policy of the Soviet Union of raising oil prices charged to their Eastern European allies to approach the world-market level (even though internal COMECON oil prices remained somewhat below that level). The possibility of a future oil shortage in the Soviet Union itself prompted the Kremlin leadership to make it known that it expected efforts by the Eastern Europeans to obtain some oil outside of the bloc as well.[3]

At the same time, conditions in the Middle East proved germane to increased European contacts during the 1970s. Many of the regimes in the area moved considerably toward the Left, thereby establishing at least a minimum ideological congruence with the communist leaderships in Eastern Europe. Even those Middle Eastern regimes that had little ideological affinity with socialism and communism were anti-imperialist and somewhat anti-Western, thereby enhancing the image of political and socioeconomic systems that could be accused of neither of these afflictions. And the very emphasis on anti-imperialism in the Middle East made it possible for the Eastern European states to gain access, whereas the Soviet Union had to battle its image as a potential inheritor of the imperialist role previously occupied by the major Western powers in the area.[4]

Against these possibilities and necessities of increased Eastern European involvement in the Middle East must be posited the liabilities surrounding the efforts of East Berlin, Warsaw, Prague, Budapest, Bucharest, Sofia, and Belgrade in the region. The sudden riches of the Organization of Petroleum Exporting Countries' (OPEC) moguls enabled them to buy the latest in technology; here, Eastern Europe was seriously deficient in comparison with the West. While the increasing autonomy of several Eastern European states alleviated their dependence on the Kremlin, they remained Marxist-Leninist, at least officially, and this connotation proved to be a distinct liability in many Middle Eastern regimes whose leaders remained dedicated to Islam. The fundamental turmoil that shook the region in the late 1970s further detracted from the possibilities of expanded contacts that had greeted the Eastern Europeans earlier in the decade. The willingness of the Kremlin to utilize some of the Eastern European states as frontmen in their own quest for penetration of the Middle East may have enabled some of the latter to increase their activities in the region, but it also limited their opportunities for success. Eastern European activity in the turbulent region of the Middle East in the 1970s therefore took place in a complex interaction of opportunities and liabilities, advantages and disadvantages. The results were therefore mixed, as will be shown below.

FAITHFUL AGENTS AND HONEST BROKERS:
THE DIFFERENTIATED EASTERN EUROPEAN
APPROACHES TO THE MIDDLE EAST IN THE
1970s AND EARLY 1980s

Given the complex circumstances of the Middle East and the differentiation that was emerging in Eastern European foreign policies, it is small wonder that the socialist regimes produced rather varied approaches to this part of the Arc of Crisis. Several kinds of policies can be established, and the Eastern European states may be grouped according to their congruence with the respective models.

The Faithful Agents

The faithful agents loyally subordinated their foreign policies to those of the Soviet Union and produced policies in the Middle East that were closely correlated with the Kremlin and designed to enhance Moscow's interests. The agents attempted to establish close relations with as many Middle Eastern regimes as possible for the purposes of limiting Western influence, enhancing the prestige of the Soviet Union and the entire bloc, and, in cases where it seemed warranted, for the purpose of expanding the power of leftist movements domestically. In some cases, the Eastern Europeans helped consolidate already existing leftist regimes by means of military, economic, and technical aid, as was the case in South Yemen, Iraq, and Syria. The faithful agents were primarily represented by the German Democratic Republic, Czechoslovakia, and Bulgaria.[5]

A touchstone of loyalty to Soviet policies in the region was the position taken on the burning issues of Israeli policies, the status of the Palestine Liberation Organization (PLO), and the question of Palestinian self-determination. The faithful agents all took an extreme anti-Israeli stance, loudly proclaimed their support for the PLO, and unfailingly argued for the establishment of a Palestinian state. The agents never failed to castigate U.S. policy in the Middle East, and they consistently criticized the Camp David accords as an imperialist sham. They denounced Egypt for its willingness to maintain relations with Israel, and on numerous occasions they received Yasser Arafat and other PLO representatives in grand style, thus demonstrating their commitment to statehood for the organization and its leadership. Considerable amounts of money and technical aid flowed from the faithful agents to those Middle Eastern regimes that were receptive. The East Germans were particularly active; for example, East German advisers worked alongside the Soviets in South Yemen, and Western intelligence services maintained that representatives of Pankow also helped run PLO camps for international terrorists.[6]

The Moderate Supporters

Two of the Eastern European states, Poland and Hungary, generally supported Soviet policies in the Middle East but were less vociferous in this support, and their denunciations of Israel and the United States were somewhat muted in comparison with the protestations emerging from East Berlin, Prague, and Sofia. These differences represented nuances; they reflected a tendency in Poland, strengthened as the decade of the 1970s progressed, to fashion some measure of autonomy in foreign policy. The Polish approach also reflected domestic developments, which produced considerable outspokenness among various societal groups and elites against too close a connection with the Soviet Union in foreign policy. Polish dependence upon Western credits also tended to limit the sharpness of the anti-Western campaign that was so prevalent among the loyalists in Eastern Europe.[7]

The Hungarian approach reflected the attempt by the Kadar regime to act as a conciliator within the bloc, thus reducing the friction between the loyal agents and the real autonomists, such as Romania. At the same time, there appeared to be a residue of pro-Israeli feeling in Hungary, particularly among the intellectuals, and a vociferous anti-Jerusalem campaign would therefore have been counterproductive to Kadar's attempts at domestic reconciliation as well. But despite such restraining circumstances, Budapest became more outspokenly pro-Soviet, pro-Arab, and anti-Israeli as the decade wore on, even if Kadar never quite joined the ranks of the faithful agents.[8]

The Nonaligned

Yugoslavia continued its policy of nonalignment in the Middle East during the 1970s; this was a policy with traditions dating back to the 1950s, when Tito became one of the most outspoken (and successful) promoters of nonalignment, together with Egypt's Nasser and a succession of Indian leaders. Belgrade had established favorable credentials in the Middle East because of this traditional policy, and Tito continued to exploit it with considerable vigor during the decade. The main elements of his policy included a campaign to ensure continued nonalignment in a region that was increasingly drawn into the vortex of global power interests, thanks to the stranglehold on energy supplies held by the Arab members of OPEC. Furthermore, the Yugoslavs sought to enhance their own oil supplies by means of a series of bilateral economic agreements with assorted Middle Eastern states. In pursuing this policy, Tito clearly worked counter to Soviet interests in that he attempted to reduce the influence of all major powers in the region, regardless of ideology and political system; but the Belgrade leadership went considerably beyond this, openly castigating the Kremlin for its imperialistic and dangerous policies. At the same time, Tito remained faithful to the Arabs in the Arab-Israeli conflict, and he repeatedly criticized the Israeli government for its highhandedness and its expansionism in relations with Arab states as well as the PLO and the Palestinians generally. This kind of policy continued to produce a fairly important impact for Yugoslavia in the Middle East in political matters. But at the same time, Belgrade's leverage suffered from the increased competition that Western states produced in the scramble for access to Middle Eastern oil. Once again, the mixture of opportunities and liabilities produced a complex environment in which Yugoslavia could register only limited results.[9]

The Honest Broker

Of all Eastern European systems, only Romania can be said to have acted as an honest broker, in the sense that its leadership made real efforts to act as a mediator between the Arabs and the Israelis in the continuing political struggle between these two Middle Eastern camps. Thus, Bucharest maintained diplomatic relations with Israel after the Six Day and Yom Kippur wars, whereas the other governments of Eastern Europe did not; throughout the 1970s, Nicolae Ceauşescu carried out a very active diplomacy in the Middle East, visiting many of the states of the region during the decade and receiving many of the primary leaders in the region in the same period. This activity extended to the PLO and even other political movements outside the official government structures of the Middle East. Ceauşescu apparently played a considerable role in bringing about the talks and meetings between Begin and Sadat in 1977 and subsequently.[10]

This varied Romanian policy in the Middle East was carried out for numerous reasons. It carried with it a number of risks as well as opportunities. First of all Ceauşescu was playing to the hilt his self-imposed role as peacemaker in the region, while also expanding the influence of Romania in world and regional politics; this was in complete correspondence with long-standing Romanian foreign policy goals since the inception of the Ceauşescu regime. Such a policy had the beneficial effect of reducing further Romania's dependence upon the Soviet Union in interparty as well as interstate relations; Ceaușescu could enhance the prestige of the Romanian state in international affairs while at the same time promoting the interests of the Romanian Communist party (Partidul Comunist Roman [PCR]) as a major political force in a disputed region, where the Romanians could ply their favorite brand of progressivism that enhanced both Romanian nationalism and the nationalism of the local regimes. In the final analysis, this kind of policy also ran counter to the interests of the Soviet state and the Communist party of the Soviet Union (CPSU), whose interests favored closer integration of the Arab states into a Kremlin-led front of anti-imperialism.[11]

Second, this policy was designed to enhance the economic viability of the rapidly expanding industrial potential of Romania. The rigid and forced industrialization policy of the Gheorghiu-Dej and Ceaușescu regimes began to pay off in the 1970s, with rigidly expanding output of many industrial products, primarily in the heavy and extractive industries. This industrial expansion required export markets, but Romania was beset by the familiar problem of low quality and an unsatisfactory product mix, which was coupled with inadequate service facilities and problems in the supply of spare parts. These serious deficiencies reduced the possibilities for Romanian exports to the West. There was always the huge Soviet market, which was less concerned about poor quality and faulty service, but the Romanian quest for foreign policy autonomy precluded full reintegration of the Romanian economy in the COMECON. There remained, therefore, the Third World, which was desperately in need of technology and industrial goods. In the Third World, the oil-producing Arab states represented the most desirable trading possibilities because Romania found itself ever more dependent upon imported fuels for its burgeoning but inefficient (and therefore fuels-consuming) industries. This economic rationale for Romanian policy in the Middle East became even more pronounced toward the end of the decade, and it culminated in the severe fuels crisis in the summer of 1979, when much of Romanian transport wound down as a result of serious oil shortages and stringent emergency measures adopted by the Ceaușescu regime.[12]

If economic rationality and the quest for increased foreign policy autonomy had been the only motivating factors in Ceaușescu's decision making for foreign policy, Romania could have adopted a distinctly pro-Arab stance in the Arab-Israeli conflict. This was not done, however, primarily because of a genuine streak of idealism, coupled with considerable realpolitik in the leadership, and particularly in Nicolae Ceaușescu himself. The PCR leader appeared genuinely committed to the role of Romania as a mediator in this explosive conflict. In addition to the humanitarian goals served by such a policy, successful mediation in the region would, presumably, reduce the possibilities for great-power involvement there; in this regard, the Romanians shared the Yugoslav quest for reduced Soviet and U.S. influence in the strategic region. Nicolae Ceaușescu went even further, however; his refusal to sever relations with Israel and his many conciliatory efforts in the area were also designed to earn the gratitude of the West, and particularly the United States, since in the correct estimation of the PCR general-secretary, only Washington's continued interest in Romanian foreign policy autonomy could help secure it. Thus, the complicated mix of idealism and realism that is characteristic of Romania's Middle Eastern decision making in the 1970s produced, in turn, a varigated and flexible policy in the region throughout much of the decade.[13]

SPECIFIC POLICIES: BUCHAREST AND
BILATERAL RELATIONS IN THE MIDDLE EAST

During the 1970s the Ceaușescu regime made certain distinctions between the various states of the Middle East on the basis of the foreign policy interests of Bucharest, the issues at hand, and the opportunities for policy influence that existed in varying degrees in the region. In some cases, the PCR leadership attempted to enhance Romania's economic interest, the foreign policy autonomy of the Romanian state, and Ceaușescu's ambition to be known as a genuine peacemaker all at the same time; in other countries, only one of the objectives was targeted. Taken together, these policy approaches represented a complicated and sophisticated policy in a troubled region.

Israel, the PLO, and Middle Eastern Peace:
A Special Problem

During the 1970s Romania labored mightily to enhance the prospects for peace in the Middle East by maintaining and enhancing its contacts with one of the sides to the problem, namely, Israel. Romania was the only Eastern European communist-ruled state that did not terminate diplomatic relations with Israel after the 1967 war, and thus, Bucharest maintained access to the Israeli leadership at a time when other states in Eastern Europe tended to follow an unequivocal pro-Arab line (in accordance with Soviet policy in the region). But the mere existence of diplomatic relations between Bucharest and Tel Aviv-Jerusalem was in no way indicative of the Ceaușescu approach to the thorny problem of war and peace in the Middle East; Romania in fact exercised an extraordinary activity in the region during the decade, a considerable part of it in bilateral talks and meetings with

Israeli officials, either in Romania or in Israel. Thus, top leaders of the various Israeli cabinets visited Bucharest during the decade (including Shimon Peres, Menachem Begin, and a succession of Israeli foreign ministers),[14] and high Romanian officials traveled to the Israeli capital on a frequent basis. In fact, such high-level meetings took place at least once a year during the entire decade, and at times, the pace of deliberations picked up even further, as for example, during late 1973 and in 1974 in the aftermath of the Yom Kippur War and during the last two or three years of the decade, when the Romanian leadership stepped up its efforts to gain international agreement on the need for a new conference on the Middle East, in which Romania could be expected to play a considerable role.[15] At times, the bilateral relations between Romania and Israel were preceded or followed by talks with representatives of Egypt, Iraq, Syria, Jordan, or the PLO clearly for the purpose of maintaining and expanding a dialogue between the two sides to the conflict through Bucharest. As the conflict in Lebanon between Muslims and Christians heated up in the second half of the decade, with resulting Syrian and Israeli involvement in that troubled country, there were more frequent consultations with Lebanese officials as well. There can be little doubt that Nicolae Ceauşescu and his government attempted to maintain a role of mediator in the Middle Eastern conflict, even though the Romanian leader frequently disavowed any such role.[16] In fact, Ceauşescu clearly had some part in the relative rapprochement between Israel and Egypt that resulted in the talks between the two leaderships and the famous meetings between Menachem Begin and Anwar Sadat, with subsequent peace agreements between these two erstwhile combatants.[17]

Efforts of mediation in the Middle East clearly could not succeed without close relations between Romania and the main confrontationist states of the region, primarily Syria, Iraq, Jordan, and Egypt, as well as the PLO itself. Throughout the entire decade, Bucharest succeeded in maintaining rather close contacts with these four states and the PLO, despite the fact that the Romanians also had relatively close ties to Israel. This kind of multifaceted relationship was an extraordinarily difficult task, and its successful maintenance certainly testifies to the skill of Romanian diplomacy; but it is also in part attributable to the perceived self-interest of the Arab states and movements involved. In Arab eyes, Romania, maintaining relations with the parties to the Middle Eastern conflict, also exhibited considerable autonomy in its relations with the Kremlin while at the same time frequently communicating with the West, including the United States; such an intermediary was a valuable asset for the regimes in Damascus, Amman, Baghdad, and Cairo, as well as for the PLO itself, insofar as the Arabs feared isolation from the West and

the ensuing reliance on the Soviet Union. As the Kremlin leadership
became more assertive in international politics throughout the decade
of the 1970s, even such leftist regimes as the Syrian and the Iraqi
leaderships began to fear the closeness of the Soviet bear's embrace
and sought to liberate themselves from the closeness of that relationship while still maintaining access to Soviet arsenals. Sadat, of
course, terminated much of the Soviet link in Egyptian foreign policy
and turned decisively to the West, but the shrewd Egyptian leader realized that no real Middle Eastern political settlement could be feasible
without some Soviet involvement, and Romania and Nicolae Ceauşescu
could provide a link with the major communist powers without undue
influence over Egyptian decision making. Thus, domestic conditions
in the confrontationist states facilitated an active role for Romania
in the region.[18]

The hectic pace of Romanian-Israeli relations was matched by
the frequent contacts between Bucharest and the capitals of the major
confrontation states. During the decade of the 1970s, Nicolae Ceauşescu visited Cairo and Damascus several times, and a number of high-
level Egyptian and Syrian officials likewise traveled to the Romanian
capital for important consultations. Iraq and Jordan were also included in these negotiations, albeit somewhat less frequently than presidents Sadat and Assad and members of their cabinets.[19] All in all,
Romania became the most active Eastern European state in the complex set of political interactions that marked Middle Eastern politics
during the turbulent 1970s. The PLO occupied an ever-expanding
role in Romanian policy in the Middle East. During the decade of the
1970s, the PLO established a permanent office in Bucharest, and
Yasser Arafat paid visits to the Romanian capital. On his frequent
trips to the Middle East, Nicolae Ceauşescu frequently met with PLO
representatives in various Arab capitals. And throughout the decade,
Romania was a faithful supporter of the PLO's interests in international forums such as the United Nations. Toward the end of the
decade, Arafat could claim that Romanian material aid had been quite
substantial; this kind of aid included medicines, money grants, and
perhaps weapons and ammunition.[20]

Changing Policy Emphases

Throughout the decade, certain basic aspects of Romanian policies in this field of activity remained constant, while others underwent
some changes, which in many cases amounted to mere nuances; in
other aspects, there were discernable changes. Among the most important constants were the following:

1. Throughout the entire decade, Romania emphasized the need for Israel to evacuate occupied Arab land. Bucharest staunchly supported the various resolutions produced by the United Nations and consistently urged the implementation of Resolution 242, which essentially did call for just such Israeli withdrawal.[21]

2. Nicolae Ceauşescu remained dedicated to the principle of a Palestinian state; as the decade wore on the Romanian leader increasingly stressed that such a state should be led by the PLO. To balance this view, Romanian policy makers also maintained the right of all states in the area to existence, hence also the right of Israel to exist as a state, with secure borders, based on the lines prior to 1967.[22]

3. The Romanian leadership emphasized the need for self-determination, national sovereignty, and independence for all states in the region. This was a mainstay of Romanian foreign policy generally, but it took on added meaning in the Middle East, where both the United States and the Soviet Union became more deeply involved during the decade. Romania was, in fact, conducting a policy that helped reduce the influence of any major power in the region, a policy that ran counter to the interests of the Soviet Union, Romania's primary ideological ally and the leader of a military pact of which Romania was a founding member. The quest for foreign policy autonomy, so consistently pursued elsewhere by the Bucharest leadership, was also very visible in the Middle East.[23]

4. Romania steadfastly argued that any solution to the Middle East problem must be a peaceful one, and Nicolae Ceauşescu went to great lengths to help ensure such a development. As discussed elsewhere,[24] the Romanian leader helped arrange the first meeting between Anwar Sadat and Menachem Begin (even though the extent of the Romanian involvement is not fully known), and Bucharest made strenuous efforts to keep a dialogue going throughout the decade. In furtherance of this policy, Ceauşescu also condemned terrorism and military reprisals against terrorist attempts, and the PCR leader made several attempts to renew and further the process of negotiations between the primary contestants, either multilaterally or, as discussed above, through bilateral discussions between Romanian officials and representatives of one of the parties concerned.[25]

During the decade, there were occasionally changes in policy; some of these changes were important enough to represent a discernible trend. One of these was the swing toward a more clearcut pro-Arab position, which was triggered by the oil embargo of 1973, the successful use of the oil weapon by OPEC, and a more militant stance by the Arab boycott office, which temporarily included Romanian firms on their lists because of continued political and economic ties between the Romanians and the Israelis. Examples of this subtle, but important, policy change include the Romanian decision to terminate oil shipments from Iran across Israeli territory,[26] more determined efforts to promote the cause of the PLO,[27] and increasing demands for Israeli withdrawal from occupied Arab territory (while the formula had previously been withdrawal from territory occupied in 1967, it later became withdrawal from all occupied Arab territories).[28] Romanian criticism of Israeli policy also became more strident after the decision of the Begin government to expand Jewish settlements on occupied land.[29]

These changes, which temporarily soured the relations between Bucharest and Jerusalem, never brought the contacts to the breaking point, and bilateral ties between the two capitals picked up again after 1976, and especially after the improved relations between Egypt and Israel and the signing of the Camp David accords.[30] During the last years of the 1970s, and also during the first year of the new decade, Bucharest continued its frantic pace of bilateral relations in the Middle East undaunted by the continuing problems of Jewish settlements on the West Bank, the political revolution in Iran, the Iraqi-Iranian war, and, very recently, the flaring up of the conflict in Lebanon once more. Thus, even the Israeli attack on the Iraqi nuclear reactor at the beginning of June 1981 failed to dislodge Romania from its self-established role as Middle Eastern mediator; true, the Romanian leadership condemned the raid, but relations with Israel were maintained, and the PCR leader once again emphasized the need for negotiations instead of armed conflict.[31]

ECONOMIC POLICY IN THE MIDDLE EAST: LIBYA, IRAN, KUWAIT, SAUDI ARABIA, AND IRAQ

Throughout the 1970s the Romanian leadership was confronted by an inescapable economic fact of the highest importance—domestic oil resources were no longer sufficient to supply the rapidly expanding industrial base of the country, and the large Romanian refineries demanded considerable import of crude in order to operate anywhere near optimum capacity. The Romanian chemical industry, which ranks among the largest and most highly developed in Europe, producing export articles badly needed for acquisition of hard currency, became heavily dependent upon imported oil for its continued operation. This undesirable situation produced a series of dilemmas for the political leadership without any clearcut and desirable solution. Conservation was rather ineffective in the short run, since areas where stringent measures could have an immediate effect, such as private automobile driving, were not highly developed in Romania, whereas heavy industry, where energy wastage was considerable, could not easily and quickly be refitted to consume less. This dilemma produced another set of rather undesirable alternatives for the regime; essentially, the choice was between expanded domestic production or increased import. Since many of the Romanian wells had been exploited for a considerable period of time, their productivity was low, and prospecting for new sources did not produce immediate results of any magnitude.[32] Out of this situation arose a third dilemma, revolving around the choice of suppliers for the imports needed. Clearly, the cheapest source would be the Soviet Union, but dependence upon Moscow for such a vital commodity was politically unacceptable in Bucharest until late in the decade, when the flow of Iranian oil was reduced.[33] The other source of imported oil was OPEC, but here the Romanians ran into the stumbling block of facing the burgeoning price rises and the requirement that oil be paid for in hard currency.

The problems outlined above necessitated a sophisticated policy on the part of the Romanian leadership. Basically, Ceauşescu and his cabinet attempted to deal with the problem by promoting barter trade between Romania and the chief oil suppliers, principally Iran, Iraq, Libya, and Kuwait. After the Iranian revolution, these efforts were extended to Saudi Arabia as well. Furthermore, the Bucharest leadership promoted technology transfer to the OPEC states in return for Arabian crude, and there were many attempts to establish joint production facilities in assorted Arabian states or in Romania itself. One of the most heavily publicized of the latter was the planned Romanian-Kuwaiti refinery at Navodari on the Black Sea coast, which was to have a 49 percent ownership by the Kuwaitis. This project, incidentally, foundered (at least up to the present) on Kuwaiti insistence that the oil provided for the project be priced and paid for in dollars and carried to the refinery in Kuwaiti tankers.[34]

The Romanians experienced varied luck in their attempts at barter trade, technology transfer, and joint projects. The best relations were established with Iran under the shah; in this case, the Iranians were willing to accept Romanian goods in exchange for oil, and the Romanians also cooperated closely with various economic units in Iran in joint ventures. Romanian oil-drilling technology and equipment were used fairly extensively in the Iranian fields, even after 1973. This rather close economic cooperation also carried with it the need for political consulting, and the shah or his top aides visited Romania several times during the decade, while Ceauşescu regularly stopped in Tehran on his many travels in the area; lower-level leadership cadres from both sides conferred frequently throughout the decade.[35]

The close political and economic relations between Tehran and Bucharest were temporarily cut off by the Iranian revolution, and they were only restored with a great deal of effort and difficulty. Romania now learned of the dangers of becoming overly dependent upon unstable political regimes. Much of the period since 1979 has been spent in attempting to restore good relations with the Khomeini regime, and it appears that this effort was crowned with success in 1981, when it was announced that Iran had agreed to supply Romania with at least 1 million tons of crude—albeit at high, world-market prices.[36] Once again, this success of Romanian diplomacy was made possible by the stringent Western boycott of Iranian oil and other products after the taking of the U.S. hostages—a fortuitous circumstance that, nevertheless, put Romania in the awkward position of acting as blockade buster and thus possibly earning the enmity of the West, which still remained an important trading area and an indispensable supplier of advanced technology to Romania.[37]

Throughout the decade, Bucharest attempted to diversify its supply of crude oil, and Libya, Iraq, and Kuwait became prime Middle Eastern targets of such a policy. Once again, the primary emphasis was on barter, technology transfer, and joint ventures. Unfortunately for Romania, all three of these regimes proved less receptive to such approaches than the shah's Iran, and in many cases, Bucharest was forced to purchase oil from these three states at world prices and with payment in hard currency. Trade with these three states nevertheless expanded greatly during the decade, and Ceauşescu did succeed in establishing a number of economic agreements that included the selling of Romanian exports and know-how in exchange for oil. Large numbers of Romanian experts worked abroad during the decade, a good number of them in Arab countries, and thousands of foreign students, including many Arabs, obtained education in Romanian institutions. In some cases, Romanian experts even provided training for military cadres, some of them from the oil-rich Arab states discussed here.[38]

The increased dependence of Romanian industry on Arab oil as well as the increased competition for this resource required a substantial political investment by the Romanians during the decade. Trips to Iraq, Libya, and Kuwait became standard items in Ceauşescu's repertoire of traveling diplomacy, and his lieutenants in the party and in the government conducted the complicated, detailed negotiations needed to establish and maintain the flow of oil across the Mediterranean and the Black Sea.[39] Despite setbacks and heavy costs, Bucharest did manage to keep the flow open, thereby ensuring the continued supply to heavy industry, the lifeblood of the Romanian economy. Under the circumstances, this was no mean achievement.

ECONOMICS AND THE POLITICAL KEYSTONE STATES: ROMANIAN ECONOMIC RELATIONS WITH EGYPT, SYRIA, AND JORDAN

While the Ceauşescu regime focused on Israel and the major confrontation states, Egypt and Syria, for political purposes, and while attempting to improve relations with the primary oil producers in OPEC for economic reasons, three countries—Egypt, Syria, and Jordan—were singled out for special attention because of their strategic position in the Arab-Israeli conflict and their economic needs. None of these three countries represented a particularly attractive economic target for Bucharest; they were relatively poor, had little oil, and could not hold up their end of the economic relationship with Romania; throughout the decade, they ran a heavy deficit in their exchanges with Bucharest most of the time. But the very economic needs of these three states made it possible for Nicolae Ceauşescu to attempt to expand his political influence in Damascus, Cairo, and Amman by means of economic assistance and leverage. Because of this use of economic relations as a political lever, Romanian relations with the Egyptian, Syrian, and Jordanian leaders are perhaps the most interesting elements of Ceauşescu's Middle Eastern policy.

The economic needs of Syria and Egypt were many and complicated, and Romania expended a great deal of money and energy during the 1970s in economic aid, technology transfer, and joint ventures. In Syria there was a project designed to exploit phosphate deposits, several agricultural cooperative ventures, irrigation schemes, and a great many smaller projects. In Egypt, irrigation schemes and some other agricultural activities as well as industrial cooperation and considerable technology transfer headed the list. Romanian trade with both countries showed a considerable export surplus for Bucharest, and in addition to this imbalance, some of the trade that actually did take place was financed by Romanian credits, thereby further increasing the economic burden of the relationship for the Romanians.[40] And despite considerable efforts by the Ceauşescu leadership, Romania apparently did not succeed in obtaining Syrian or Egyptian oil.[41]

The primary reason for the continuation of this rather unfavorable economic relationship for Romania was (and is) predominantly political, not economic. Extensive economic relations with the two key states in the Arab-Israeli conflict allowed Romania direct access to both sides of the controversy in a manner that would not have been possible otherwise, and it therefore enhanced the possibility of fulfilling the function of honest broker in the troubled region of the Middle East. Nicolae Ceauşescu utilized this position to the fullest. His contacts with presidents Sadat and Assad were more substantial, more imbued with strategic and geopolitical overtones, than the other relationships forged by Bucharest in the region. It was primarily through his ties with the Egyptian president that Ceaușescu could help foster a rapprochement between Jerusalem and Cairo; the PCR leader's friendship with President Assad helped defuse the dangerous confrontations between the Syrians and the Israelis on the Golan Heights and in Lebanon. This is not to suggest that Romania was the most important factor for a measure of stability in the Middle East, but it was one factor of some impact. The policy of increased political influence through expanded economic relations was the primary reason for this success of Romanian diplomacy. [42]

During the last few years, the ties between Romania and Egypt have apparently been expanded into areas that had previously been overlooked or considered unnecessary. Reports have hinted at a fairly close military relationship between Bucharest and Cairo; such reports are, however, difficult to substantiate, and the extent of such cooperation cannot be determined. They do seem plausible, given the rather frequent contacts that have been enjoyed by the two military establishments during the 1970s in the form of official visits. [43]

Relations with Jordan were also carried out by means of the economic carrot, which in turn provided Ceaușescu with better access to King Hussein and other Jordanian officials. Throughout the decade, Romanian trade with Jordan increased substantially; but, once again, Bucharest exported much more than it imported, and some of this trade, too, was financed by credits. Some joint ventures, primarily in irrigation, were established. [44]

The economic strategy pursued by the Ceaușescu regime in Jordan accomplished its primary objective, which was to establish better political access to the leadership of one of the confrontation states. Because of the strategic location of Jordan, its claims on the West Bank, and its erstwhile ties to the PLO, it was readily understood in Bucharest that no solution to the Palestinian problem could be achieved without Jordanian cooperation. This fact, together with King Hussein's reputation as a moderate in the Arab world with good contacts to both Washington and Moscow, made the Jordanian leader a prime target for Ceaușescu's efforts as honest broker. This special position was reflected in the communiqués emanating from the various meetings of the two leaders and their subordinates in the many meetings that took place during the 1970s. This high level of contact has continued up to the present. [45]

CONCLUSION: THE LIMITED SUCCESSES
OF THE HONEST BROKER

After more than a decade of hectic Romanian activity as an honest broker in the Middle East, it is possible to make an assessment of the successes and failures of this policy. First of all, it is clear that both the achievements and the setbacks of Romanian policy in the area should be seen in the context of Bucharest's means and the possibilities that emerged in the region itself. Second, Romania, as a medium-sized power, necessarily possessed only limited opportunities to influence the politics and economics of the Middle East, since the global powers became heavily involved in the region prior to the 1970s and remained committed to an active policy there during the decade in question; in fact, the vital importance of this oil-producing region further increased the concerns of policy makers in Washington and Moscow over developments there. In short, the future of Israel and its Arab neighbors as well as the Persian Gulf states and others hinged upon decisions made in the major capitals of the world, not in Bucharest.

Given the limits and parameters within which the Ceaușescu regime had to operate, its achievements were considerable. Bucharest did manage to establish itself as an honest broker in the turbulent region, and as such it had direct access to both sides in the Arab-Israeli conflict—a position not shared by any of the other Eastern European states. This status was maintained despite considerable handicaps; after all, a state that maintained diplomatic relations with Israel and even traded rather extensively with the Jewish state would not normally obtain much of a hearing in the Arab capitals; and, by the same token, a founding member of the Warsaw Pact would not necessarily gain access to Israeli decision makers. The reasons for Romanian access to both sides was clearly the understanding in virtually all capitals of the region that Bucharest in fact had considerable autonomy in foreign policy, was genuine in its efforts to promote peace and reconciliation, and did maintain contacts with both Washington and Moscow. Once this understanding had been achieved, the way was paved for Nicolae Ceaușescu and his lieutenants to play an active and constructive role in the region.

From the Romanian vantage point, an active policy in the Middle East was a logical continuation of the traditional Romanian quest for foreign policy autonomy—a quest that has been conducted in the Warsaw Pact and the COMECON, in European affairs, and in Africa, Asia, and Latin America. During the 1970s, however, the Middle East became particularly important for Romania in economic terms as well. The entire development strategy of the Romanian modernizers during the last 35 years has focused on extensive, forced, and rapid industrialization, which depended very heavily on ample energy supplies. Once these supplies reached depletion domestically, it became important to secure substitutes abroad, and the Middle East became a logical target for the Romanian buying spree in oil. At the same time, this region offered potential markets for the increasing flow of industrial goods coming on line in the rapidly expanding economy of Ceauşescu's Romania during the 1970s. The highly versatile, active, and imaginative policy of Bucharest in the Middle East therefore came about as a result of domestic economic needs as well as the ideological view of Ceauşescu and the traditional autonomist tendencies of Romanian foreign policy makers.

The assessment of this complicated policy must be a positive one. The Romanian quest for a position of honest brokerage did contribute to the tenuous peace of the region. In the economic sphere, Bucharest did manage to secure vital oil supplies from the Middle East. And in the overall scheme of Romanian foreign policy, relations with the states and movements of the Middle East added considerably to the autonomist quest, which has now become a standard element of Ceauşescuism. This is indeed a success story of rather impressive dimensions, despite the frustrations of occasionally experiencing exclusion from the councils deciding the future of the region, and despite the heavy economic costs of doing business with OPEC while failing to unload massive amounts of industrial products at favorable prices. As the 1980s get under way with the new challenges of a new decade, there must be a measure of genuine satisfaction in Bucharest as Nicolae Ceauşescu and his lieutenants contemplate their Middle East policy of the preceding decade.

NOTES

1. A good overview of Soviet policy in the Third World generally can be found in Elizabeth Kridl Valkenier, "The USSR, the Third World, and the Global Economy," Problems of Communism, July-August 1979, pp. 17-34.

2. For a fairly detailed discussion of these dynamics, as well as a survey of existing literature on the subject, see, for example, Andrzej Korbonski, "The 'Change to Change' in Eastern Europe," in Political Development in Eastern Europe, ed. Jan F. Triska and Paul M. Cocks (New York: Praeger, 1977), pp. 3-30.

3. Several of the Eastern European states scrambled to get such supplies during the 1970s; see, for example, Radio Free Europe, Bulgarian Situation Report, January 13, 1977 (hereafter cited as RFE), on Bulgarian efforts; see also Vanshna Targovia (Sofia), no. 12, 1977, on Bulgarian imports of Libyan oil. Hungary also has an agreement to buy Libyan oil, but little has been procured owing to the high price of Libyan crude. As for Poland, imports from key countries such as Iraq stood at the level of 2 million tons in 1980; see RFE, Polish Situation Report, November 21, 1980. Czechoslo-

vakia imported 3 million tons from the Middle East in 1978; see RFE, Czechoslovak Situation Report, February 7, 1979.

4. Ceauşescu emphasized this aspect of Romanian policy in his proposal for a conference of developing countries; see Scinteia, March 29, 1977.

5. I have derived this analysis from an examination of the Eastern European press, Radio Free Europe analysis, and the existing literature. For an examination of Soviet goals and objectives in the Middle East, see the following articles in Problems of Communism: David Lynn Price, "Moscow and the Persian Gulf," March-April 1979, pp. 1-14; John C. Campbell, "Communist Strategies in the Mediterranean," May-June 1979, pp. 1-18; Edward J. Agar, "Soviet and Chinese Roles in the Middle East," May-June 1979, pp. 18-31; and Elizabeth Kridl Valkenier, "The USSR, the Third World, and the Global Economy," July-August 1979, pp. 17-34.

6. For example, Michael Ledeen and Arnaud de Borchgrave, "Terrorism and the KGB," Washington Post, February 17, 1981.

7. Derived from a study of the local press, for example, Glos Pracy (Warsaw), November 17, 1977, commentary on President Sadat's visit to Israel.

8. Magyar Hirlap (Bucharest), November 22, 1977, on the Sadat visit.

9. One of Yugoslavia's problems was increased competition for leadership in the nonaligned movement (especially from Cuba and other pro-Soviet states) and the resulting fissures in that movement. An example of this Yugoslav concern is an article in the weekly Nin (Belgrade), June 17, 1979.

10. Specific evidence on this point is not directly available, but there were hints of such developments when Ceauşescu visited Egypt in May 1977 and Sadat returned the visit in late October of the same year. For reports on these visits, see Scinteia, May 12, 13, and 14, 1977, and October 29, 30, and 31, 1977. Menachem Begin also visited Bucharest in the later summer of 1977; see ibid., August 30, 1977. Ceauşescu's views on the Middle East were further elaborated in an interview with Israeli journalists in ibid., September 13, 1977. In February 1977, President Assad of Syria was in Romania; see ibid., February 15, 1977.

11. Soviet interests have been analyzed in Agar, "Soviet and Chinese Roles."

12. The problems of energy shortages were discussed by Nicolae Ceauşescu in a speech to industrial and construction officials in Scinteia, March 7, 1979.

13. This policy is set in the framework of Romanian foreign policy generally; see Ceauşescu's opening speech to the Twelfth PCR Congress in ibid., November 20, 1979.

14. Menachem Begin also visited Bucharest in what is now considered an important meeting with Ceauşescu that helped pave the way for the Sadat visit to Israel. For a report on the Begin visit see ibid., August 30, 1977.

15. One of the first statements on the Romanian position came in an article commenting on the Yom Kippur War in ibid., October 20, 1973.

16. For example, Ceauşescu during his visit to Egypt in May 1977; see ibid., May 14, 1977.

17. See note 10 for details on the flurry of visits to Bucharest as well as Ceauşescu's traveling diplomacy during the period preceding the Sadat visit to Israel in November 1977.

18. A general analysis of the political and socioeconomic conditions in the Middle East and Soviet and Chinese approaches can be found in Edward J. Agar, "The USSR, China, and the Middle East," Problems of Communism, May-June 1979, pp. 18-34.

19. The list of contacts was nevertheless high. For example, Romanian Foreign Minister George Mascovescu visited Iraq in April 1973; RFE, Romanian Situation Report, April 26, 1973. King Hussein of Jordan visited Romania in January 1974; ibid., February 4, 1974. Ceauşescu visited Iraq (as well as Syria and Lebanon) in February 1974; for example, Scinteia, February 22, 1974. Ceauşescu visited Jordan in April 1975; RFE, Romanian Situation Report, April 24, 1975. In the same month, a delegation from the Iraqi Communist party visited Bucharest; Scinteia, April 26, 1975. Paul Niculescu, Romanian deputy prime minister, visited Iraq in July 1978; RFE, Romanian Situation Report, August 1, 1975. King Hussein was again in Bucharest in February 1980; Scinteia, February 20 and 23, 1980.

20. The communiqué issued after Arafat's December 1979 visit to Bucharest (for talks with Ceauşescu) discussed, among other matters, the training of Palestinian cadres in Romania; see Scinteia, December 8, 1979.

21. For example, Ceauşescu in ibid., July 10, 1979, reporting on his discussions with UN Secretary-General Kurt Waldheim in Bucharest.

22. Ibid.

23. The Romanians even refused to sign a document emanating from the East Berlin conference of communist leaders, July 3-5, 1979. This document opposed the peace settlement between Egypt and Israel; see RFE, Romanian Situation Report, August 8, 1979.

24. Ibid., December 23, 1977; see also note 10 above.

25. As early as 1976 the Romanians argued for a conference on the Middle East in which all interested parties could participate; for example, in Romania Libera, January 23, 1976.

26. RFE, Romanian Situation Report, March 15, 1976.

27. For example, a communiqué issued after Arafat's visit to Bucharest in late 1979 in Scinteia, December 8, 1979.

28. Ibid.

29. Such concern was rather forcefully expressed in a communiqué issued after Premier Manea Manescu's visit to Syria in March 1978; see ibid., March 18, 1978.

30. An example of this was the first quarter of 1978, when Israeli Foreign Minister Moshe Dayan visited Romania (April). He had been preceded by Eliahu Ben Ellissar, a special envoy from Menachem Begin, in January. Furthermore, the Israeli ambassador to Romania became very active in meetings with Romanian officials at this time. This round of activities was capped by a visit to Bucharest by the Israeli Mapam party, reported in ibid., March 2 and 3, 1978, and a visit by Shimon Peres, head of the Israeli Labor Alignment, reported in ibid., March 15, 1978. See also RFE, Romanian Situation Report, April 17, 1978.

31. Ceauşescu's speech to the second conference of workers' councils, in Scinteia, June 25, 1981.

32. Ceauşescu reported oil findings in the Black Sea in his report to the Twelfth PCR Congress, but there has been very little publicity about this since then, indicating disappointing results of the drilling efforts there. Ceauşescu's address to the congress can be found in ibid., November 20, 1979.

33. The flow of Iranian oil to Romania was resumed in 1980, after negotiations between Iranian officials and Romanian leaders, for example, Ion M. Nicholae, deputy minister for foreign trade and international economic cooperation in the Romanian government; reported in ibid., March 7, 1980. Soviet exports of oil to Romania are discussed in RFE, Background Report no. 135 (Eastern Europe), June 9, 1980.

34. The arrangements for the petrochemical complex were reportedly negotiated throughout the 1970s; see, for example, reports on meetings between Romanian and Kuwaiti officials in Kuwait in Scinteia, February 14, 1978.

35. These contacts were among the most important Romanian ties to the Middle East and the Persian Gulf, and the shah was treated with a great deal of pomp and ceremony during his visits to Romania. For an example of this, see the report in the Romanian press of the shah's visit to Bucharest in June 1973. For an extensive report on the visit, see ibid., June 2, 1973.

36. This agreement was forged in various meetings between Romanian and Iranian officials; reported in ibid., March 7, 1980.

37. For a thorough discussion of the Romanian oil problem, see Patrick Moore, "Romania: The Cost and Politics of Oil," RFE, Background Report no. 255 (Romania), November 23, 1979.

38. Of even greater interest is the training of PLO cadres in Romania; the communiqué issued after Yasser Arafat's visit to Bucharest in December 1979 spoke of such training; see Scinteia, December 8, 1979.

39. In order to safeguard such supplies, Ceaușescu constantly needed to maintain good relations with the frontline states in the Arab-Israeli dispute. During the decade, the Romanian leader expanded his contacts with such hardliners as Assad of Syria and Arafat of the PLO for just this purpose. An example of this is Ceaușescu's visit to Syria in August 1979. For detailed reports, see ibid., August 14, 15, 16, 17, and 18, 1979.

40. These credits were substantial even by the middle of the decade; RFE, Background Report no. 180 (Romania), December 22, 1975, discussed a number of such credits to Egypt, totaling several hundred million dollars, while credits to Syria had amounted to about 200 million by then. Most of these credits were issued for the purpose of selling Romanian machinery and finished products to Egypt and Syria.

41. One of the items of negotiation during the August 1979 visit by Ceaușescu to Syria was the expansion of the Banias oil refinery and possible deliveries of Syrian oil to Romania. For the text of the final communiqué of the visit, see ibid., August 18, 1979.

42. Some economic experts disagree with the costs of this policy, and this sparked a debate in Romanian media, for example, ibid., August 4, 1978.

43. Many Egyptian military leaders have visited Romania, and Ceaușescu and Sadat became close friends, as evidenced by the Ceaușescu visit to Egypt in May 1977. The communiqué issued at the end of the visit spoke of close relations and cooperation in many fields; see, for example, ibid., May 14, 1977. Also see ibid., May 12 and 13, 1977, for extensive reports on the visit.

44. The joint communiqué issued after King Hussein's visit to Romania in February 1980 also spoke of the desirability of further cooperation in such fields as drilling for water, cement production, and the development of the chemical industry; see Agerpres, February 23, 1980.

45. Ibid.

11

SOVIET POLICY IN THE MIDDLE EAST: IN SEARCH OF ANALYTICAL FRAMEWORKS

VERNON V. ASPATURIAN

SOVIET INTERESTS IN THE MIDDLE EAST

The Middle East, including the Eastern Mediterranean area, is a region where Soviet interests as a global power intersect with Soviet security and defense interests, important domestic interests (that is, Soviet nationalities policy), and to an increasing degree, economic interests (that is, energy resources). As a region that is adjacent to the southern Soviet periphery where two Caucasian republics and four central Asian republics border on four states (Turkey, Iran, Afghanistan, and China), it would seem to be of extraordinary importance to the Soviet Union. Yet until about 1955, the Middle East, of all the regions proximate to the Soviet Union, received the lowest priority in the calculation of Soviet leaders. Today the Middle Eastern region often assumes center stage in Soviet foreign policy calculations and increasingly becomes a point where the risks and dangers of confrontation with its two most implacable global rivals, the United States and China, are the greatest.

Soviet fortunes in the Middle East, indeed as those of other major powers, have fluctuated widely. As recently as in 1977, the astute Egyptian journalist Mohammed Heikal, could write with consummate and apodictic self-assurance that

> by this summer of 1977, there can be no escaping the realization that the entire Middle East Policy of the Soviet Union is in ruins. There is not a single country in the whole area which can be considered a true friend, let alone a reliable ally. Whereas a few years earlier the Soviet Union had been everywhere regarded as the principal defender of Arab rights, today it is to Washington that

all roads from the Arab world lead. To rub salt in the
Soviets' wounds is their realization that if, at this particular
moment, there is any prospect of their once again
playing a significant role in the decision-making processes
of the Middle East, this will only come about as a result
of American invitation to do so.[1]

Even some Soviet commentators were so demoralized by the
prospects for revived Soviet influence in the region after Nasser's
death and Sadat's ejection of the Soviet presence on the Nile that the
shah's Iran—the United States' local surrogate—was grudgingly recognized
as a model of political stability and socioeconomic progress,
an indirect tribute to the primacy of U.S. influence in the region.
Thus, according to a Soviet specialist on the Middle East, writing in
1975,

Iran is one of the few Third World countries that have experienced
a marked change in their economic and social
indices over the past ten years or so. Her success is due
to very diverse factors, not least the effective use made
of natural resources, the obvious adaptation of ruling circles
to the country's new internal situation, a realistic
foreign policy that recognizes the importance of good-
neighbourly relations with adjacent states, and lastly,
her relative demographic stability. Her achievements
have attracted the attention of the governments of a number
of Asian countries, who are now trying to adopt some
of the methods being used in Iran.[2]

By 1980 the entire situation in the Middle East had been radically
transformed, and the Soviet Union appeared suddenly on the
verge of engulfing the entire Persian Gulf region and its rich oil resources.
While Heikal was celebrating the downfall of the Soviet position
in the Middle East and its failure to find or develop a single reliable
client state or regional surrogate, and while Soviet Middle Eastern
specialists were hailing the shah's Iran as a model of social stability,
political prudence, and economic progress, the major assumption
upon which these analyses rested—sustained U.S. power and perceived
willingness to use it—was disintegrating. Although the ineffective
response of the United States to the armed Soviet-Cuban intervention
in Angola in 1975 could have been recognized as a harbinger of
future U.S. reaction to Soviet behavior in other parts of Africa, which
had a low priority in U.S. foreign policy and security calculations, it
was totally unexpected that the United States would behave in approximately
the same manner to changing events in the Persian Gulf region,

an area explicitly recognized as a region of vital interest for the United States, Western Europe, and Japan. The Carter administration's general passion for avoiding confrontation appeared to be amply signaled, however, when the Soviet Union and Cuba shifted the focus of their military intervention from the Atlantic side of southern Africa to the Horn of Africa, an area intimately connected culturally, geographically, and strategically with the Middle East.

And when the shah's regime was undermined and threatened from within, the Carter administration similarly betrayed an unexpected indifference to the fate of its admittedly erratic and difficult but nevertheless most important and generally loyal client in the Middle East. The Carter administration, while seriously and paralytically divided over the best course of action and unable to distinguish between the unacceptable and undesirable in its policy choices, on the whole appeared to be more concerned with the tarnished human rights credentials of the shah's regime than with the consequences of upheaval and the establishment of a fanatically anti-U.S. clerical dictatorship whose human rights violations would exceed even those of the shah.

The low-risk international environment created by the Carter administration, coupled with growing Soviet capability to project power in various parts of the world, increasing self-confidence and self-assurance on the part of the Soviet leadership, and the development of new dangers as well as opportunities, congealed to virtually invite the Soviet military intervention in Afghanistan. The only bright spot in the gloomy Middle Eastern scenario that was unfolding was the Sadat initiative resulting in the Camp David process and the rapprochement of Egypt and Israel, a development, however, which was subsequently endangered by Sadat's assassination.

Thus, even before the first year of the new Reagan administration had been completed, the Soviet Union enjoyed a foothold in Angola, a presence in Ethiopia, a toehold on the Arabian peninsula (South Yemen), and a Soviet-occupied Afghanistan. Iran's animosity toward the United States and the bizarre war with Iraq effectively isolated Iran from its former protectors, while the Soviet invasion of Afghanistan encircled it on three sides, with Soviet troops arrayed in a wide northern arc from the Caucasus to Baluchistan. Unable to resolve the war with Iraq and further embittered toward the United States, the reactionary Muslim-fundamentalist clerical regime was rendered vulnerable to Soviet threats and blandishments. The prudent Soviet regime cleverly offered assistance and inducements rather than threats, calculating that in spite of the wide ideological gulf between Moscow and Qum, under the existing circumstances the Khomeini regime could be enticed into choosing the lesser Satan over the greater in the conviction that it could manipulate Moscow against the United States. As a result, a limited but wary cooperative relationship appears to be developing between the two countries that is mutually beneficial to both, at least temporarily.

This arrangement serves to deter a possible U.S. military intervention in Iran, which neither Moscow nor Iran wants for different reasons; Soviet gestures of friendship toward Tehran undercut the notion of a Soviet military threat to the Persian Gulf region while simultaneously conjuring up at least the appearance of a possible Soviet protective mantle against further U.S. threats and pressures.

The region, however, remains as volatile as ever, and can once again change dramatically. This derives largely from the inherent internal social and political instability of local regimes and the unresolved Arab-Israeli conflict, which further aggravates the instability. Moscow has adjusted to the realities of the region and no longer searches for a reliable and permanent client state as an instrument of its penetration but, rather, pragmatically and expediently associates itself with various countries whose interests may transiently parallel those of Moscow. These arrangements can be short-lived (Iraq, for example), drawn out but episodic (Syria), unpredictable in duration (Libya), traumatic (Egypt), and contingent (Iran). The reduced presence of the United States and increased power and leverage of the Soviet Union in the region lessen the immediate need for an ideologically reliable ally or client state as an instrument of penetration, although Moscow would probably feel more confident of successful penetration if an authentic, ideologically reliable, and politically stable Marxist-Leninist (or socialist-oriented) regime could be established in a major Middle Eastern state. Iran emerges as the most likely candidate for a variety of reasons.

1. It is politically and ideologically isolated.
2. It is surrounded and encircled by Soviet military power.
3. The regime's social and political stability is fragile at best and is vulnerable to internal pressures, including terror directed at the clerical leadership.
4. The regime's legitimacy is untested, since it rests entirely upon the personal authority of Khomeini, whose actuarial future is bleak.
5. The presence exists of a durable, experienced, socially anchored, and well-organized pro-Soviet, Marxist-Leninist party (Tudeh), which is ready to assume power with Soviet "fraternal assistance."

The dramatic turnaround in Soviet fortunes in the Middle East has revived with renewed force conflicting appraisals of Soviet intentions and behavior in the Middle East and in the world at large. The conflicting estimates resolve themselves not only in different models and theories of Soviet behavior in the Middle East but also into different contexts and levels of analysis, which correspondingly assign different priorities to the Middle East in Soviet foreign policy calculations.

THE GRAND-DESIGN AND TARGETS-OF-OPPORTUNITY MODELS

In analyzing Soviet policy and behavior in the Middle East, several explicit and implicit analytical models have been employed, two of the most conspicuous being the grand-design and targets-of-opportunity models. Other models that have been employed are those that emphasize Soviet security, defense, and military considerations, and Soviet domestic imperatives, including internal factional maneuvering, elite interests, economic needs, and nationalities policy. Needless to say, we can only touch upon each of these models in brief or cursory fashion.

The grand-design model concentrates on Soviet long-range goals and purposes, within which individual Soviet moves and actions are located and plotted. It is a model that is inspired and informed by both ideological and traditional Soviet imperialistic imperatives and interests and correlates very well with the growing global military capabilities of the Soviet state. Soviet foreign policy moves are not examined in isolation from one another as if they were responses to local situations or induced by specific issue imperatives but, rather, are viewed as interconnected with past Soviet moves and possible future Soviet action. Thus, while the Soviet-Cuban intervention in Angola in 1975 seemed to some to be somewhat remote from Soviet policy in the Middle East, those who subscribe to the grand-design model might point out that the significance of Angola for the Middle East was anticipated by the Soviet leaders who could see its connection to East Africa, which in turn is linked to the Middle East. With the invasion of Afghanistan in 1979, only four years after the Angola intervention, the proponents of this model argue that together with the intervening events, this validates the notion that Soviet behavior in Africa and the Middle East was part of a deliberate envelopment strategy and that the only unplanned elements were timing and specific events, neither of which can be predicted but can be taken advantage of if one is primed to expect such events to take place.

The targets-of-opportunity model, on the other hand, is based on the assumption that no specific Soviet grand design, master plan, or global strategy exists, and that these models are simply new variants of the old discredited world-communism or world-revolution models of analysis. Soviet behavior is perceived as largely reactive in character rather than initiatory, and the inherent social instability and political volatility of the Middle East consigns any predetermined grand design to futility. Soviet policy, it is argued, is pragmatic and flexible, largely unideological in character, and cleverly attuned to the transitory and unpredictable character of the behavior of the local states. What the Soviet Union is primed to do is to take advantage of events and opportunities as they unfold, tailoring its behavior to specific situations rather than behaving in a predetermined fashion. This accounts for the ebb and flow of Soviet activity in the region and the changing priority of the Middle East in overall Soviet foreign policy calculations; it accounts for the almost frivolous manner in which Moscow shifts from client to client, arming various states indiscriminately, including those that are clearly unreliable, unstable, and likely to betray Moscow. This mode of activity suggests the priority of short-term advantages and ad hoc goals, rather than a grand design. In short, it emerges as the Soviet variant of muddling through.

Obviously, there is something to be said in favor of both models. It is unnecessary to assume that Soviet intervention in Angola, Ethiopia, and Afghanistan constitutes a Soviet grand design or global strategy to recognize that the Soviet Union has developed a global policy to correspond with its as yet modest global capabilities. There is neither an overall Soviet master plan (grand design) nor a five-year or ten-year plan (global strategy) in foreign policy but, rather, a global policy that results from the intersection of Soviet global capabilities and residual universalist ideological goals. In the recent past, ideological goals were modified and placed in cold storage, largely because it was counterproductive to orchestrate them too vocally and because the Soviet Union did not have the capabilities to implement them. If Soviet global capabilities continue to grow and those of the United States wane, we can expect a resurgence of Soviet ideology as a shaper of Soviet foreign policy.

An ominous indication of this trend is an apparent Soviet decision to give a global and universalist application to the so-called Brezhnev Doctrine. If any doubts about the dimensions and character of Moscow's global policy and its possible reideologization existed, they should have been dissipated by the unusually imperious speech made in April 1980 by the Soviet ambassador to France, S. C. Chervonenko (the same Chervonenko who staged and orchestrated the massive intervention of Czechoslovakia in 1968 from his vantage point as Soviet ambassador to Prague). Even today the Soviet interpretation of the Brezhnev Doctrine and its application remain a mystery. While it surely applies to the Warsaw Pact states and perhaps the socialist commonwealth, the exact dimensions of the latter have never been unambiguously defined, and whether Moscow intended it to apply to China, Yugoslavia, Albania, and other marginal communist states was never made clear. Ambassador Chervonenko's speech goes a long way in answering this question and explaining the precise mechanics of how its application is set into motion. Chervonenko warned in connection with the Afghan invasion that the Soviet Union "would not permit another Chile," a rather imperious and arrogant pronouncement in itself, and made the extraordinary statement that, now, any country in any region anywhere on the globe "has the full right to choose its friends and allies, and if it becomes necessary, to repel with them the threat of counter-revolution or a foreign intervention."[3]

This expanded Brezhnev Doctrine not only justifies the invasion of Afghanistan but retroactively justified the Cuban-Soviet military intervention in Angola and the Horn of Africa, and it poses an immediate threat to Iran or any other country where internal chaotic conditions can generate invitations to Moscow for support to quell internal counterrevolutions or external intervention. The invitations to Moscow from Prague in 1968 and Kabul in 1979 provide sufficient cause for concern that the Soviet leaders are not overly fastidious in examining their invitations and are fully capable of inviting themselves should no invitation be forthcoming. To give a further global dimension to his remarks, Ambassador Chervonenko gratuitously warned that the Soviet Union would not recognize an assertion by the United States that the Persian Gulf or any other region was a special area of vital interest to it and that any such claim would be contested. The Soviet ambassador emphasized the claim to equality with the United States not only as a military power but also as a global power and contended that the Soviet Union had an equal right to be consulted and involved everywhere in the world on all major issues, with the implicit threat to intervene to claim and assert such a right.

All this strongly suggests that Soviet policy amounts to something less than both a grand design and global strategy, and yet is something much more than responses to targets of opportunity. The Soviet invasion of Afghanistan was clearly an initiatory act and not a reactive one. Even more important, its demand that, in advance of any definition or occasion, as an equal to the United States it must be consulted in principle on all major issues everywhere hardly seems like a passive, reactive policy that a targets-of-opportunity hypothesis would convey. The Soviet Union responds to targets of opportunity; it often creates its own opportunities; and it behaves in the absence of opportunities.

The Soviet move in Afghanistan must be linked with earlier and continuing Soviet-Cuban moves in Africa. As former White House National Security Adviser Zbigniew Brzezinski has pointed out, there is an Arc of Crisis stretching along the western edge of the Indian Ocean from Mozambique to Pakistan. This Arc is probably more the product of U.S. unwillingness to support its local clients than of the Kremlin's political diplomatic engineerings. Soviet initiative in virtually all parts of the Arc has been missing. The revolutions in Mozambique, Ethiopia, North Yemen, and Afghanistan were the result of indigenous activity to which the Soviet Union responded, usually following an invitation from a new regime or one of the factions in an internal civil struggle. And one can hardly blame Moscow for the upheaval in Iran.

Nevertheless, the overall consequences of Soviet behavior within a global context may eventually be indistinguishable from the execution of a grand design. And the opportunities that have inadvertently and fortuitously been created may induce the Soviet Union to behave as if in accordance with a grand design or to create one to take systematic advantage of the situation.

INTERNAL FORCES AND PRESSURES

But, even the targets-of-opportunity approach appears to be too all-encompassing to other analysts who maintain that both of these models presuppose Soviet behavior to be the product of a unitary rational actor, when in fact the Soviet leadership is often divided over the best course of action, and that Soviet behavior must be analyzed accordingly in terms of specific domestic elite interests and concerns, of which military, nationality, and economic are the most evident. Furthermore, current Soviet Middle Eastern policy must be put into proper historical context in order to understand the learning process that the Soviet leadership has experienced and how this, in turn, has given rise not to a single, rational perception of Soviet interests and priorities but often to competing and conflicting perceptions.

Soviet interest in the Middle East and Eastern Mediterranean has been long, durable, and persistent. In spite of unrelenting attempts to establish a presence in the area over the past century in concert, association, or intrigue with a wide assortment of other powers, until comparatively recent times all of these attempts have resulted in signal failure for one reason or another. Neither the alliance with the Entente in World War I, nor the ill-fated association with Hitler in 1939-41, nor the joint Allied victory in World War II could bring about the realization of a more-than-100-year ambition to become a Mediterranean and Middle Eastern power. All of the USSR's partners, of whatever political hue, ideological coloring, or vintage, seemed equally implacable in blocking Soviet entry into this vital waterway, which has always been of strategic importance to Europe, Asia, and Africa and now plays a crucial role in the overall global balance of strategic power. One need not go into detail concerning the various stratagems employed by Moscow to reach into the Mediterranean and Middle Eastern area, since this has been amply covered elsewhere. The following analysis will deal almost exclusively with the internal forces and pressures that have impelled the Soviet Union to expend the immense effort, resources, and risks to achieve status as a Mediterranean and Middle Eastern power and also with the impact that these policies have in turn had upon the interplay and interaction of domestic forces inside the Soviet Union. Only passing reference will be made to the goals and objectives—both short-term and long-range—of Soviet policy in this region, and attempts will be made wherever possible to link them with domestic sources of impetus and feedback effects upon Soviet domestic institutions, forces, and entities.

Initially, Soviet objectives in the Eastern Mediterranean and the Middle East were primarily ideological in character, stemming largely from Moscow's self-assumed mission of encouraging and supporting revolutionary movements and groups of various hues as they struggled to free themselves from European economic and political control and influence. Fledgling communist parties, radical nationalist movements, and reformist, anticolonial regimes, including monarchies, were supported in various ways in Turkey, Iran, Afghanistan, and elsewhere soon after the revolution in an endeavor to simultaneously erect a political buffer zone against outside intervention and provide a foundation for further ideological penetration and expansion. While Soviet policy during this period was largely bereft of explicit strategic and commercial and political goals in the traditional sense, as the Soviet regime stabilized itself and grew in strength, the activities of the Comintern and its various external components in these countries became de facto instruments of traditional Soviet purposes in the area, although within the context of world communism and deliverance from colonialism and capitalism rather than Czarist expansion or Christian humanitarianism. The establishment of Soviet power in the Transcaucasus and its formal incorporation into the USSR once again made the Soviet Union a Near Eastern, if not an Eastern Mediterranean, power, and the traditional imperatives of security interests in the region once again assumed their cardinal importance. Commercial and economic interests in the region were also soon resurrected, and ideological interests were thus simply grafted upon those already ordained by geography and history.

From 1924 to 1939, Soviet interest in the Eastern Mediterranean and the Middle East was largely passive in character. It had no active or affirmative policy, since its limited capabilities compelled it to focus upon the more crucial areas of central Europe and the Far East. An active Eastern Mediterranean policy was simply a luxury that the Soviet Union could not afford, since the British and French presence in the region seemed firmly entrenched and fixed. The opportunities for penetration and influence were sparse, and the possible benefits of such a policy equally meager.

SOVIET POLICY IN THE MIDDLE EAST / 135

The Nazi-Soviet pact and the first phase of World War II, however, created unexpected opportunities and possible windfalls. The collapse of France and the military isolation of a beleaguered Great Britain appeared to presage an imminent collapse of the Anglo-French sphere of influence in the Eastern Mediterranean, threatening to create an enormous vacuum, which Stalin felt should be shared by Hitler. Less than a year before the German attack upon the USSR, a bizarre conference took place between Molotov and Hitler in Berlin in which the German dictator offered to define the forthcoming Soviet sphere of influence in the region by expansively suggesting that Moscow focus its attention in the general direction of the Indian Ocean, a vision too grandiose and remote to have any relevance for Moscow's real concerns, which at the time were in the Balkans and Turkey. The Soviet response to this offer contained, among other <u>desiderata</u>, a demand for a Soviet military and naval base on the Turkish Straits, while the horizon that Hitler offered Molotov was lowered to more accessible regions. "The center of the aspirations of the Soviet Union" was defined as being "south of Batum and Baku in the general direction of the Persian Gulf" in the formal Soviet reply to Hitler's more generous but less realistic offer. Berlin apparently rejected the Soviet counterproposal by never replying to it.

The Nazi-Soviet negotiations thus revealed that the traditional interests of the USSR in Iran, Turkey, and the Straits had lain dormant but were not dead and at least strongly suggested that Soviet ambitions in this region could easily be aroused if the opportunity presented itself; but they equally suggested that Moscow was in no position to elevate them to a primary or high-priority interest.

The Allied victory in World War II, the collapse of German and Italian power in the Balkans, and the weakening of the British position, however, served to sustain the opportunities at a level sufficient to impel Stalin to at least make a serious effort to extend Soviet influence not only in Iran, Turkey, and the Straits, but also to Greece, North Africa, and even East Africa. Different stratagems were employed in each case, defined largely by the conditions, circumstances, available instruments, and credible justifications. In Iran Soviet military pressure, exerted mainly through Moscow's refusal to withdraw its forces from nothern Iran, combined with the establishment of a puppet autonomous regime in Persian Azerbaijan and the manipulation of the leftist Tudeh party were used in an effort to extract economic and possibly territorial concessions from Tehran. In Turkey, where neither a viable communist party or leftist movement existed, Stalin employed Georgian and Armenian irredentism to annex territory from Turkey in the East and relied upon the support of grateful Allies to coerce Turkey, which had wavered and vascillated during the war, into permitting the Soviets to establish military and naval bases on the Straits. The traditional Soviet obsession with security and free exit from the Black Sea were offered as principal justifications. In Greece a civil war instigated by local communist militants, although apparently neither initiated nor enthusiastically sanctioned by Stalin, was reluctantly co-opted by Moscow.

Ironically, it was the local Communist attempt to move Greece into the Soviet orbit that was the principal factor that mobilized and congealed Western sentiment against the otherwise reasonable claims that Moscow made against Turkey, although the Soviet debacle in Iran also played its role. As part of an apparent concerted design to establish itself as a Mediterranean power, the Soviet Union also unexpectedly made bids of varying degrees of effort to become the trust power in three former Italian colonies: the Dodecanese Islands off the Anatolian coast, the Cyrenaican part of Libya, and in Eritrea on the Horn of African. All three bids were rebuffed in spite of Molotov's eloquent appeals that the Soviet contribution to the Allied victory, its well-known opposition to colonialism, and its long experience with nationality problems made Moscow eminently qualified to become a trust power. In addition, Moscow demanded one-third of the Italian navy as war booty, presumably to use it as the basis of a Mediterranean fleet.

All of the postwar Soviet attempts to establish itself in the Eastern Mediterranean region failed. Had the Soviet Union succeeded across the board, there is little question but that Moscow would have become a Mediterranean power of some magnitude, given the fact that the British were already expressing their inability to fully preserve their former presence and were calling upon the United States to fill the vacuum. The eventual upshot was the emergence of the United States as a Mediterranean power and the incorporation of Greece and Turkey into the Western alliance system as U.S. protectorates. Stalin prudently retreated to the Black Sea, and after his death his successors made amends to Turkey and officially withdrew his earlier demands for both bases and territory.

Down to about 1947, the role of internal forces, institutions, and groupings in the shaping of Soviet policy in the Eastern Mediterranean, as well as the impact of such policy upon the domestic situation, was rather limited and restricted. Private interest groups in the Soviet system that could conceivably develop a vested interest in the region did not exist; nor, with the exception of the armed forces, were there any public institutions sufficiently independent or functionally differentiated to develop discretely distinguishable, even though nonconflicting, interests in the area. The armed forces, particularly the navy, was anxious to secure free exit from the Black Sea, and the addition of new territory south of the Caucasus would undoubtedly improve the Soviet defense perimeter in that vital region; but, aside from this, there was little opportunity or even perception of separate interests by Soviet public bodies and institutions. Furthermore, the Soviet decision-making process was so centralized during this period that Soviet public bodies and institutions were largely instrumentalities of the decision makers rather than active participants in the decision-making process. Whatever benefits accrued to various internal public bodies, institutions, or groupings were largely fortuitous windfalls and not the product of conscious pressure, leverage, or even design. Thus, had Stalin's postwar demands in the area materialized, the armed forces, particularly the navy, would have been substantially benefited whether it actively participated in formulating the policy or not.

Policies in the region as elsewhere were largely conceived and developed within the leadership, based upon its values, goals, and definition of interests, and similarly executed in accordance with its judgment and assessment of the situation.

These interests were broad and diffuse in character and did not correspond in a discrete sense with the specific interests of given interval entities. Rather, the overall purpose was to strengthen the Soviet Union and to expand its power and influence to ensure, in the first place, the security and survival of the Soviet state, and to prepare, in the second, a foundation for expanding the area of Soviet influence via conventional means or the spread of communism. Moscow sought bases on the Turkish Straits and territory in eastern Turkey largely for strategic and defensive purposes, although eventually they could be used as a basis for further expansion. In Iran Moscow sought not only oil concessions on favorable terms but wished to weaken the Iranian state and draw it into the Soviet political orbit. In Greece ideological aims were imposed upon (but accepted by) Moscow by local communist militants. And Soviet demands for trust territories in Africa could be described essentially as a desire for enhanced international prestige and acceptance, although such trust territories would enable Moscow to establish a foothold in Africa as a prelude to undermining British and French power in the continent.

Stalin prudently refrained from making demands that would explicitly encroach upon established French and British interests, and thus the Arab states were considered off-limits for the moment.

As Soviet power grew and that of the United Kingdom and France waned, some Soviet leaders perceived an opportunity to fill in at least part of the vacuum that was being created by the departure of the British and French. Middle Eastern policy became a controversial issue within the leadership, since the initiatives proposed by Khrushchev threatened to feed back and affect the domestic political and social equilibrium of forces within the Soviet Union itself. The intimate involvement and commitments to noncommunist, bourgeois-nationalist radical regimes raised important ideological and party issues, while the logistic problems of enforcing an overseas foreign policy threatened to upset the internal equilibrium among the various branches and services of the military. Furthermore, taking the Arab side in the Arab-Israeli conflict would seriously affect Soviet Jews and Muslim nationalities and perhaps upset the entire nationality equilibrium in the Soviet Union.

The continuing and deepening involvement of the Soviet Union in the Middle East since 1955 has resulted in interlacing specific domestic interests with policy in the area. The Communist party apparatus, various sectors of the economy, Jews, Muslims, Armenians, Soviet Turkic groups, the armed forces, sociofunctional groups, and even factions within the state bureaucracy—all, to some degree, have developed a vested stake in Soviet policy in the Eastern Mediterranean. While it is exceedingly difficult to causally relate the interests of specific groups with certain aspects of policy, it would appear that, as in the case of religious and national groups, the influence upon the shaping of policy and the reciprocal impact of policy upon interests is both uneven and fluctuating in character. Individual Soviet leaders and factional groupings within the leadership have also developed a vested stake in the Soviet Middle Eastern enterprise that would seem to affect their political fortunes favorably or adversely. The minor shake-up in the Soviet Central Committee after the 1967 Arab-Israeli war, coming immediately upon indications in the Soviet press of a bitter controversy over the implications of the Arab defeat for the USSR, and similar changes after 1973 suggest this very strongly.

Individuals closely associated with Alexander Shelepin and Nikolai Podgorny in particular appear to have suffered a loss in influence within the leadership. The precise contours of these factional lines, together with their positions, cannot be fixed, but it appears certain that the 1967 and 1973 wars affected some individuals and groupings adversely, while benefiting others. Similarly, controversy over whether to maintain, diminish, or deepen the Soviet commitment to the Arab cause leaves an uneven impact upon various public institutions, factions, social groupings, and sectors of the economy. Furthermore, the general Soviet citizenry is also vitally affected by the costs of a particular policy in the Eastern Mediterranean in relation to other priorities. The Soviet Union, over the past decade and a half, has poured enormous resources into the Middle East, and thus possesses an enormous economic, military, and political investment in the region that it must protect and preserve, and the existence of this investment has been shaped by the interests of various internal forces just as it in turn continues to affect the fortunes of these domestic groups.

First and foremost, Soviet policy in the Middle East has contributed immensely to the importance of the armed forces in the Soviet system, although the armed forces may not have actively advocated such a policy in the first place. In the past 15 years, however, the Soviet military seems to have developed a vested stake in the policy that goes over and beyond simply the abstract interests of the Soviet state. The Arab defeat in 1967 was in some ways a defeat for the Soviet military, since it was charged with equipping and training the Egyptian forces. Its prestige thus suffered indirectly. The Soviet military was determined that its Egyptian client would never again suffer a similar defeat. As a result, Soviet troops, technicians, advanced military equipment, and even marginal involvement in military operations were intensified, although the death of Nasser and Sadat's expulsion of the Soviet presence ultimately resulted in the transformation of Egypt into a U.S. client. Nevertheless, the limited psychological victory of Egypt in the 1973 war with Israel can be viewed as a limited vindication of the Soviet military's prestige and reputation.

During the period of intensive cultivation of Egypt as a client state and Moscow's decision to expand into other Arab states, all branches of the Soviet military were involved in the growth necessary to support Soviet policies and commitments in the region. But it was the Soviet navy, in particular, that demonstrated the greatest relative growth as a consequence of Soviet ambitions in the Mediterranean. The expanding commitment to the Arab states has been accompanied by a steady growth of Soviet naval forces, which increasingly have assumed a key tactical role in asserting the Soviet presence in the region. Establishing a sphere of influence in the Mediterranean in effect has released the Soviet navy from its landlocked environment, enabling it to grow to meet and exploit the expanding opportunities that lie waiting in the Atlantic, the Persian Gulf, and the Indian Ocean. Since Soviet policy in the Eastern Mediterranean has justified the rapid growth of the Soviet navy, we can assume that the Soviet naval forces have developed an enduring interest in preserving and expanding Soviet power in this region. A failure of Soviet policy in the area could have disasterous consequences for the Soviet naval forces, which might be deprived of their quasi bases in North Africa and be forced back into the Black Sea, with a resultant contraction and diminished role to play in Soviet life.

The military investment in the Middle East has also affected the Soviet economy, particularly the defense industries and heavy industries. Egypt and other Third World countries have become a dumping ground for obsolete and surplus Soviet weapons. The demonstrated military ineptness of Arab armies virtually guarantees a perpetual market for surplus and obsolete weapons. It becomes a market for spare parts, and altogether Soviet policy in this region serves to keep Soviet defense industries humming and busily developing and producing new weapons, which can be tested and tried out in the region.

On the other hand, light industry, agriculture, the consumer-goods industries, and the service industries may view Soviet policy in this area with disfavor, since commitments to the Arab countries serve to drain away scarce resources and preserve economic priorities that these sectors of the economy find distasteful. This policy also arrests or decelerates their growth in spite of growing demand at home for their goods and services.

A third group whose interests are ambiguously affected by Soviet military policy is the party apparatus. Normally, this institution finds itself in close informal alliance with the military and heavy industry, but this is by no means clear with respect to the Arab states. Since none of the Arab states are communist in character and all have legally outlawed their communist parties, the purists in the party apparatus are understandably apprehensive with Moscow's extensive and expensive flirtation with regimes that are internally unstable, politically unreliable, ideologically suspect, and basically anticommunist. Local communists are often persecuted, harassed, jailed, and executed by regimes that are actively supported by Moscow. This serves to demoralize local communists, frustrate the development of communist parties, arrest agitation for Marxist-Leninist-type revolutions, and in general serves to ally Moscow with anticommunist regimes.

Furthermore, some veteran Soviet party officials are concerned that these basically bourgeois regimes are exploiting Soviet power for their own purposes and would be ready to abandon the Soviet association if more desirable options were to make their appearance. There are suggestions that some senior party officials in the USSR regard the regimes in Egypt, Syria, Iraq, Algeria, and Sudan as more fascist than socialist in character. Thus, these officials may view with alarm the fact that the Soviet Union in some ways has become the prisoner of weak, ideologically erratic, and politically unreliable client states that could inadvertently maneuver the Soviet Union into confrontations with the United States, forcing the Soviet state to lay its prestige on the line by either escalating risks on behalf of dubious goals or withdrawing in prudent humiliation.

It is noteworthy that senior Soviet party ideologists like Mikhail Suslov never expressed consistent enthusiasm for these regimes or the Soviet association with them. Unlike the organizational party types like Brezhnev, it appears that the ideological types are not particularly enthusiastic about the specific manner in which the Soviet Union is attempting to cultivate a sphere of influence in the Middle East.

Furthermore, Soviet support for regimes that outlaw local communists serves as a signal to other communist parties that they, too, can expect to be sacrificed to promote Soviet global power interests as distinct from Soviet ideological interests. This creates a possible opening for the Chinese, who may come to the rescue of local communist parties abandoned by the dictates of Soviet expediency.

RELIGIOUS GROUPS AND NATIONALISM

Aside from purely public bodies and institutions, other internal forces that were to become more intricately involved in the Middle Eastern policy of the Soviet Union were social and national groupings and, in particular, certain religious groups and nationalities. Soviet Jews, Muslims, Georgians and Armenians, and even the Russian Orthodox church had important links with the region, as well as discretely defined and perceived interests that could vitally affect Soviet policy and, in turn, be affected by it.

Thus, the Russian Orthodox church with its interests in Jerusalem and its spiritual links with Greek Orthodox communities in Greece and the Arab world, the Jews with their interest in Palestine and later Israel, the Armenians with their special ties to Armenian communities in the Eastern Mediterranean countries and irredentist claim to their historical homeland in eastern Turkey, the Georgians with similar though less extensive territorial claims to Turkish territory, the Azerbaijani and their association with neighboring kinsmen in north Iran, and the Soviet Muslims with their spiritual links with other Muslims in the Mediterranean region were all utilized as pawns of Soviet policy in one connection or another. The Armenians inside and outside the Soviet Union were energized and activated to give legitimacy to Soviet demands against Turkey, since this was a cause to which all Armenians of various political hues could rally, and the new State of Israel was quickly recognized and military assistance funneled through Czechoslovakia, which was welcomed warmly by Soviet Jewry and aroused substantial support for Soviet goals among sectors of Jewish communities abroad.

Although the potential was great, Stalin was not as skillful in utilizing Soviet Muslims as instruments of Soviet policy, partly because of the circumstances of individual cases and partly because of Stalin's own personal predisposition toward Muslim nationalities, which he viewed with a scorn just short of contempt. Furthermore, Stalin was pursuing policies detrimental to Muslim states and communities in the region, supporting Armenians and Georgians against Turks and supporting Jews against Arabs. Under the circumstances, it was perhaps more prudent not to needlessly arouse Muslim consciousness and remind Soviet Muslims of their external links. Even the Soviet activity in Persian Azerbaijan was carefully disassociated from Soviet Azerbaijani irredentism, unlike Soviet claims against Turkey that consciously inflamed Georgian and Armenian nationalism in an active manner.

Although Stalin skillfully orchestrated and controlled the active involvement of Soviet religious and national groups in support of Soviet policy, he was equally adept at circumscribing their initiatives and continued to actively repress their latent predisposition to act spontaneously in behalf of Soviet interests that happened to coincide with their own more specific interests. Stalin knew that officially inspired and directed involvement of these groups in support of Soviet interests could easily develop its own individual momentum and become dysfunctional and even dangerous to Soviet policy if events and circumstances dictated a reversal or abandonment of policies supported by these groups. Soviet Jewish support for Israel might continue even if Soviet policy became hostile to Israel, and Armenian irredentist demands against Turkey might persist even if Moscow reversed its attitude and sought rapprochement with Ankara. Stalin recognized these hazards and dangers, and he developed contingency plans to deal with them, relying principally upon instruments of terror to keep these sentiments in check.

Nonetheless, the official blessing bestowed upon the activity of selected national and religious groups in support of specific aspects of Soviet policy imparted to it a measure of legitimacy, even within the Soviet context, that could not be easily or completely extinguished. By recognizing the right of Soviet Jews and Armenians to support Soviet policy in the name of promoting and defending Jewish and Armenian national interests, Stalin inadvertently legitimized Jewish and Armenian nationalism as an absolute right. At this stage, the revival of Jewish self-identity and consciousness posed a greater hazard to Stalin's policies than did Armenian nationalism, since the Jewish state that became the focus of Soviet Jewish support was not under Soviet control or influence and seemed unlikely to be in the foreseeable future. Furthermore, the more active involvement of the more numerous and influential Jewish community in the United States on behalf of Israel and its greater importance to Israel itself impelled the suspicious Stalin to perceive the possibility that Soviet Jewry, because of its concern with Israel, might be converted into an instrument of Israeli and even U.S. interests, and he took immediate measures to frustrate and eradicate this possibility. Whether Soviet policy toward Israel assumed an ever more hostile turn during the Stalin period because of this fear of a potential fifth column or whether it stemmed from a conscious decision to abandon Israel as a possible Soviet client state in the Middle East in favor of other prospects remains difficult to discern. Irrespective of why Soviet policy toward Israel underwent an abrupt change, the consequences for Soviet Jewry of this initial exercise in becoming actively implicated in Soviet Near Eastern policy was a near calamity, which was avoided only by the fortuitous death of Stalin in 1953. The episode also contributed mightily to the recrudescence of anti-Semitism in the Soviet Union, which ultimately developed its own rationale independent and separate from Soviet policy toward Israel and yet influenced it as well as conditioned the attitude of Soviet Jews to the Soviet state itself.

It should be noted that the Soviet attitude toward the Arab states and their claims against Israel was not a factor in Soviet behavior at this time. The alienation of Moscow from Israel and the alienation of Soviet Jews from the Soviet regime became essentially a domestic problem whose dynamics assumed an independence from Soviet policy in the Middle East out of which it grew. When Moscow in 1955 developed an active pro-Arab policy, this simply aggravated the alienation, which has since grown to enormous proportions and threatens to become one of the most serious domestic problems of Soviet society. Conceivably, Jewish alienation could spread and infect other nationalities whose latent resentments and frustrations against the Soviet regime might easily be forced to surface.

The increasing Soviet involvement in Arab affairs and support for Arab claims against Israel have resulted in the activation of the Soviet Muslim nationalities, even to the extent of using Muslim political and cultural dignitaries as Soviet diplomats to Arab countries. Since none of the Soviet Muslim nationalities are Arab, not national but religious and cultural affiliation is being employed and activated. Here again, as long as Soviet policy is pro-Arab, it does not run counter to normal Soviet Muslim sentiments; but should it for some unforeseen reason become anti-Arab and hence indirectly anti-Muslim, some alienation of Soviet Muslims can be expected owing to this particular aspect of Soviet policy.

Changes in Soviet policy toward Turkey also resulted in a similar cycle of mobilization and alienation of Armenian support for Soviet causes in the area. As long as Soviet claims against Turkey, ostensibly on behalf of the Armenians, were not abandoned even though not vigorously prosecuted, there was little reaction from the Soviet Armenians other than varying degrees of gratitude and support. After Stalin's death, however, when his successors formally apologized to Turkey and forced the Georgians and Armenians to officially abandon their irredentist claims, Armenian disenchantment gave way first to disillusionment and eventually to potential alienation as the Soviet regime actively sought to detach Turkey from the North Atlantic Treaty Organization (NATO) and its alliance with the United States. As part of this effort, the Soviet regime, in response to Turkish representations, has sought to muffle those aspects of Armenian nationalism that appear offensive to the Turks. Thus, in 1965 and 1966, when the Armenian Republic commemorated the fiftieth anniversary of the Turkish massacres, Moscow intervened to downplay the event. The consequence was anger and revulsion, which erupted in demonstrations and riots in Yerevan as Armenian speakers attacked the Turks and demanded that the Soviet authorities do more to satisfy their claims against Turkey. These anti-Turkish sentiments were publicly expressed by outstanding Armenian intellectuals, writers, and scientists of unimpeachable loyalty to the Soviet state and fidelity to the Communist party. As a result, changes were dictated from Moscow in the leadership of both the Armenian Communist party and government because of their inability to control these exuberant manifestations of nationalism; but these resentments and anger continue to persist.

It should also be pointed out, however, that the new Soviet approach to Turkey has found a warm reception in Soviet Azerbaijan and among the various Turkish nationalities in central Asia, all of whom have strong cultural, linguistic, and religious ties with the Ottoman Turks. Thus, if Moscow should once again adopt a policy hostile to Turkey in response to Armenian pressures or for some other reason, it runs the risk of alienating the Soviet Turkish nationalities, who in the meantime, have been mobilized to support and facilitate Soviet rapprochement with Ankara and Soviet policy in the Arab East.

The following points are important in this connection by way of summary:

1. National and religious groups in the Soviet Union have become converted from passive objects of manipulation by Soviet leaders into increasingly active pressure groups seeking to force Moscow to adopt policies in the Near East that are congenial or at least not hostile toward states and groups that have close connections with them. In almost all cases, this poses a serious dilemma for the Soviet authorities, since domestic Soviet national and religious groups pressure the Soviet regime on behalf of contradictory policies. Responding to Jewish demands in support of Israel would alienate Muslim nationalities, whereas responding to the pressures of Muslim nationalities to support the Arabs against Israel and to seek rapprochement with Turkey will continue to alienate Soviet Jews and Armenians.

2. The Soviet regime is involved currently in a serious conflict with substantial numbers of Soviet citizens because its policies in the Middle East have aggravated anti-Semitic tendencies at home. To a lesser degree, Moscow is in danger of alienating a significant number of Armenians because of its refusal to actively press Armenian national claims against Turkey. The Armenians pose less of a problem than the Jews because they are more vulnerable as a national entity— virtually the entire Armenian nation resides on Soviet territory—and thus they enjoy no option aside from displaying their resentments, anger, and frustrations in symbolic and passive form. In the case of the Jews, the Soviet Jews constitute only a small fraction of the total

world Jewish community, and the Jewish state exists outside Soviet control. Jewish alienation thus can assume the form of increasing demands for emigration to Israel, and this agitation will find considerable support in Israel, the United States, and in other countries. Bowing to these demands in turn could complicate the regime's relations with other national and religious groups, which might demand similar rights to emigrate, particularly those national groups whose national states lie outside the Soviet Union. Furthermore, allowing Soviet Jews to leave for Israel would bring cries of outrage from Arab states, since this would have the effect of not only strengthening Israel but also reinforcing the legitimacy of Jewish claims to Palestine. Nevertheless, important as Arab sentiments may be on this issue, the Soviet Union has cruelly manipulated the issue of Jewish emigration to promote interests that have a higher priority than Soviet-Arab relations. The flow of Soviet Jews from the USSR has been determined more by the state of Soviet-U.S. relations than by Soviet-Arab relations. When Soviet-U.S. relations are good, from the Soviet perspective, greater latitude for Jewish emigration is evident; when they are bad, Jewish emigration slows down. This infuriates the Arabs, but it signifies that the Soviet Union places a higher priority on its strategic and global interests than its interests in the Middle Eastern region.

3. Soviet policy in the Middle East is now inextricably enmeshed in Soviet nationality problems at home and affects Soviet relations not only with individual Soviet nationalities but also influences the relationship of Soviet nationalities with one another as each attempts to push the Soviet regime into a direction that conflicts with the interests of the other. Even Soviet claims to Turkey under Stalin triggered Armenian-Georgian quarrels, since the two republics had overlapping territorial claims against Turkey. As a single state attempting to simultaneously represent the national interests of more than a score of different nationalities, the Soviet leaders are discovering that Soviet foreign policy goals, particularly in the Middle East, have unwittingly exposed the basic incompatibilities of Soviet nationality policy as it simultaneously attempts to discharge its obligations to various nationalities in the field of foreign policy and discovers, for example, that its foreign policy on behalf of the Armenians conflicts with its foreign policy on behalf of the Soviet Turkish nationalities.

4. The uneven impact of Soviet policy in the Middle East on various Soviet national and religious groups also involves uneven costs and risks for the Soviet regime. However, the Muslim and Turkish nationalities, while relatively numerous in both total numbers and individual nations, are not among the more intensively developed and skilled in the Soviet Union. They do, however, occupy large tracts of strategically located territory on the borders of the USSR and in-

creasingly they are becoming an important factor in the Soviet conflict with China. The alienation of substantial numbers of Soviet Muslim and Turkish citizens would thus pose a serious problem for Moscow, although the general level of consciousness among these groups is relatively low and thus the dangers are not proportionate to their numerical size. On the other hand, the Jews and Armenians are relatively small in total numbers, but they are two of the more intensively developed and skilled sectors of the Soviet population, particularly the more than 2 million Jews who constitute an invaluable, almost indispensable, human reservoir of scientific, intellectual, and artistic talent. This is also true, but to a lesser degree, of the Armenians, who in addition to supplying the Soviet Union with outstanding scientists, intellectuals, and creative artists, also furnish substantial numbers of highly trained and skilled organizational, managerial, military, and administrative individuals, operating in sectors from which Jews are excluded for political and other reasons. In short, both national groups are creative minorities dispersed throughout the Soviet Union, performing valuable and important functions. Their alienation for any reason could result in a substantial reduction in their efficiency and performance and, correspondingly, in that of the Soviet system as a whole. Jewish and Armenian interests in the Middle East are neither in harmony nor in conflict: Armenians have claims against Turkey and have no quarrel with the Arabs or Jews; Jews have claims against the Arabs and quarrels with neither Turks nor Armenians. Thus, the discussion of the cost of their alienation to the Soviet Union should not be interpreted as meaning that their pressures upon Moscow are in the same direction. They move simply in different but not opposing directions.

5. Ultimately, the greatest costs and risks that the Soviet Union may bear as a result of its Middle Eastern policy may well be the feedback effects of its changing policies upon the nationality equilibrium at home. And while the Soviet invasion of Afghanistan was not prompted primarily because of an immediate fear that Soviet central Asian Muslims might be contaminated by the Muslim fundamentalism brushing up against the USSR's southern frontiers, the impact of three Muslim fundamentalist regimes in Iran, Afghanistan, and Pakistan was a factor. The danger of Muslim disaffection from Moscow is not acute, but it is chronic and has a latent potency of which the Soviet leaders are very conscious.

THE WORLD IN THE FUTURE

Although Soviet domestic factors and concerns are much too involved for its Middle Eastern policy to be exclusively determined by external considerations, whether it be based on a grand-design or targets-of-opportunity approach or whether it be global or regional in context, recent Soviet activity in Africa, the Middle East, and the Caribbean area strongly suggest the existence of a coherent global policy within which various regional policies are related and orchestrated. The Soviet invasion of Afghanistan seems to have involved all of these internal and external variables in the decision. As Jiri Valenta has observed,

> Soviet decisionmaking on Afghanistan . . . was affected by (a) Russia's traditional search for influence in the area, (b) the precarious political situation in Afghanistan, (c) fears about domestic stability, and (d) national security and strategic considerations. The invasion of Afghanistan, like the invasion of Czechoslovakia, was designed to regain control of what was slipping away. Each was the outcome of a complex decisionmaking process.[4]

Although not yet a grand design woven out of targets of opportunity and domestic imperatives, this global policy only transparently conceals a powerful Soviet ambition to supplant the United States as the paramount international power—to become, following U.S. footsteps, its principal manager and regulator. The kind of world management and regulation that the Soviet Union promises to deliver can already be discerned in the Soviet scholarly and journalistic literature, within the context of Leninist ideas, whereby the changing correlation of forces is forcing an extensive restructuring of the international system that would be "designed to completely exclude from international relations _imperialist_ violence and threats," that is, a system in which U.S. and Western power is neutralized or nullified.

> The change in the balance of forces of the two social systems constitutes a decisive factor in restructuring the system of international relations, because this balance is a key issue determining its very nature. The weight of the socialist community in the economic, moral, political, and military balance of forces in the world today has been constantly growing, just as, on the whole, the role it plays in world politics has also increased. The foreign policies of socialist countries have become far more effective, and the coordination of their joint action in solving major issues of our day has become more close and purposeful. As soon as the balance of forces in the world began to change in favor of socialism, possibilities for establishing international relations on truly just and democratic principles were extended.[5]

Several years later, the same Soviet author candidly revealed that the kind of world regulation and management the Soviet Union will deliver is already evident within the Soviet bloc of states.

> The new style international relations that have taken shape and are developing among the socialist countries provide a convincing model of relations among nations and represent a major factor in influencing the development of the present-day world.[6]

When overall Soviet behavior is viewed within this context, one can begin to understand the Soviet determination to expand and diversify its strategic arsenals beyond its defense and security needs and why it pursues a flexible ideological policy with the Eurocommunists in Western Europe, the do-it-yourself Marxist-Leninists in Africa, and the variegated nationalist and revolutionary movements throughout the Third World, as well as a motley assembly of traditional and conservative regimes sprinkled around the globe. Whether this ambition is fulfilled will depend upon the changing domestic situation in combination with perceptions of possible U.S. countermeasures and reprisals and the overall changing balance of resolution and power between Moscow and Washington, upon which both Soviet initiatives and reactions are ultimately based.

Such a design should not be confused with the crude ideological design of earlier years formulated within the context of world revolution or world communism. Revolution and communism will be supported and promoted only in areas where it is supportable and promotable. As the paramount global power, the Soviet Union would seek to make necessary and appropriate adjustments to both the developed capitalist world and the underdeveloped Third World, and although the Soviet Union would coordinate and manage all three worlds, it would pursue distinct and separate policies toward each.

The establishment of effective control or political predominance in Iran could go a long way in finally confirming the Soviet Union as the paramount power in the international system. Unlike Egypt, Iran is not geographically remote from the center of Soviet power and lines of communication and transportation. Once Soviet control, whether through direct military means (which is unlikely) or through internal subversion via the Tudeh party (more likely), is established in Iran, it is likely to be permanent. In the process, of course, Iran could be converted into a larger and more serious Afghanistan problem, but the Iranian prize is of such magnitude economically, strategically, and psychologically that, once the decision is made to incorporate Iran into the socialist commonwealth of nations, Moscow will spare no effort in ensuring success.

NOTES

1. Mohammed Heikal, The Sphinx and the Commissar (New York: Harper & Row, 1978), p. 13.
2. O. Dreyer, Cultural Changes in Developing Countries (Moscow: Progress, 1976), p. 9.
3. As quoted in the New York Times, April 22, 1980.
4. Jiri Valenta, "The Soviet Invasion of Afghanistan: The Difficulty of Knowing Where to Stop," Orbis, Summer 1980, pp. 215-16. Compare also Vernon V. Aspaturian et al., The Soviet Invasion of Afghanistan: Three Perspectives, UCLA, Center for International and Strategic Affairs, ACIS Working Paper no. 27 (Los Angeles: CISA, 1980).
5. N. Kapchenko, "Socialist Foreign Policy and the Restructuring of International Relations," International Affairs, April 1974, p. 5.
6. N. Kapchenko, "Leninist Foreign Policy: A Transformative Force," International Affairs, October 1978, p. 7.

PART V

CONCLUSION

12

THE AUTONOMY TALKS: MIDDLING THROUGH

JAMES LEONARD

INTRODUCTION

It is axiomatic of the problems of the region that the most perplexing issue of the Middle East, the question of Palestinian autonomy, should have been left as the last chapter of this volume. It shows clearly that in spite of its obvious importance—and clearly the question of what to do with, or even whom to designate as, the Palestinians remains one of the toughest issues of the area—the problem of the Palestinians remains unresolved and is viewed by many as insoluble. And yet, if the United States expected to be an honest broker in the Middle East peace process, we had to tackle the problem and deal with the issue as mediators between Israeli and Arab interests.

It was also axiomatic that the U.S. negotiating team for the autonomy talks had to walk a narrow middle line between the Israeli and Egyptian concepts of autonomy. To do otherwise would be to bring our usefulness in the mediatory role—which history has, for our sins, delegated to the United States—to an end. But how to locate the middle? It could not be a mechanical halfway point between the Israeli and Egyptian positions on issue after issue, regardless of the substantive merits of either position. Our views would have no weight with either side unless they had a solid basis in law, in equity, and in political reality. Yet we could not simply declare the U.S. position on one issue after another as it arose. Doing so would diminish or destroy our ability to work constructively with the party whose position was further from ours in developing better proposals and selling them to his principals. For Americans, who temperamentally like to say forthrightly where they stand, this timid mediatory role was exceedingly frustrating; the paucity of concrete results after more than 18 months of effort was worse than frustrating. And yet, the patience, the sensitivity, and the integrity of the members of the U.S. team were such, at least in the view of this observer, that these frustrations were never expressed in an inappropriate way. The experience was an instructive and moving one, and the U.S. response to it (as we kept telling ourselves) at least held things together and kept a difficult situation from getting a great deal worse.

This chapter does not attempt to recount and analyze the substantive course of the negotiations. Rather, it addresses the most basic of questions—how the parties came to hold the views that they hold. Without a firm understanding of this aspect, it is not possible to formulate sound and constructive judgments on how progress might be made.

The author of this chapter is not a Middle Eastern expert. A number of his colleagues are; and perhaps, if what follows shows any sensitivity to the human dimensions of a great contemporary drama, it can serve as a tribute to his teachers, those much-maligned experts in our negotiating team, in our embassies in Tel Aviv and Cairo, and in what is sometimes thought to be the innermost fortress of amorality and cynicism, the U.S. Department of State.

NEGOTIATING PEACE

The U.S. negotiating team for the autonomy talks spent somewhat more time in Israel than in Egypt. In our view there was good reason for dividing our time unevenly: there are at least three parties to these negotiations besides the United States. Two of them, the Israelis and the Palestinians, were accessible to us from Tel Aviv, whereas in Cairo we were talking only to Egyptians. We speak of the Palestinians as a party; unhappily they did not come to the table, but we tried to be in touch with their thinking, on which some comments are offered below. First, however, let us discuss the Israelis and their position on the question of Palestinian autonomy.

Living in Israel is a very intense and moving experience. This is a nation of survivors and children of survivors. And what they survived is one of the most horrifying passages in all recorded history. Among the leaders of Israel, there are quite a few sabras, or native-born Israelis; but among the general adult population the sabras are a minority. The character of Israel today is still set by the refugees from Europe and the anti-Semitism of Hitler or Poland or Russia or the Balkans. A staggering share of these former refugees lost parents, brothers, sisters, children, cousins, perhaps every relative they had in the world in Hitler's death camps. Among the hundreds of Israelis we knew, these massive tragedies were the norm; to have one's family more or less intact was so extraordinary as to seem almost miraculous.

A second large group of Israelis—numerically now the largest element—is made up of the refugees and children of refugees from Arab countries. Their memories of life in the ghettos of Iraq or Yemen are, at best, bittersweet memories. Thus, most Israelis today are refugees conditioned by often horrifying experiences in their younger years or, if they are under 30, by the horrifying experiences that their parents have recounted to them.

Regarding the sabras, who might be thought to have grown up under conditions somewhat like those considered normal by most Americans, What in fact has been their life experience?

A sabra of about 60 would have grown up during the Palestine mandate of the 1920s and 1930s, when each year was more violent, more bloody, than the year before. Arabs and Jews were fighting each other, commingled with Arabs fighting the British and Jews fighting the British as well. Then, in high school or college years, this sabra would have joined in one of the Jewish units that fought the war of independence. A younger sabra, born in the 1940s, would have lived through four more wars after independence, separated by short intervals of peace—intervals punctuated by constant war scares and terrorist incidents, and, at most, 11 years long.

As one small illustration of what life has always been like for Israeli parents, I recall an evening when my two daughters who were visiting in Israel came home from a day of sightseeing. They had had lunch in a café on the main street of Tel Aviv and during their lunch had watched the bomb squad deal with a bomb in the café across the street. It was interesting for the children. It was worrisome, to put it mildly, for the parents. Such incidents are a constant reminder of the profound truth that the ends do not justify unjust and inexcusable means.

Most visitors are struck by another fact relating to this atmosphere of tension from which no Israeli can really escape: it is the guns. Travelers who have been in a great many places remark that they have never seen so many guns as in Israel. The young men and women doing their military service are constantly carrying them along the streets, in the buses, and at the hitchhiking stations where they catch rides to and from their units. And these are not mere pistols but rifles and submachine guns.

For the visitor, the ever-present guns are one very visible reflection of the pervasive concern about surprise attack. The Israelis themselves experience this concern in a different way, through their universal military service right after high school and through the annual recall for training to which Israelis are subject for most of the rest of their lives. They are very conscious, to say the least, that they live on a sort of small island surrounded by a sea of unfriendly Arabs. Much is sometimes made of the Soviet phobia about being encircled by enemies. If Soviets can feel that way on the vast semicontinent of the Soviet Union and if the West makes much of understanding their fears, imagine how much more intense must be the Israeli consciousness of encirclement.

Much more could be said about the history and the personal experiences that have shaped contemporary Israeli views, but the best characterization of their impact is provided to a visitor, again and again, by Israeli friends. "Yes, we are paranoid," they say when tasked with having an excessively bleak, worst-case reaction to some event or proposal, "but how could we not be paranoid in the light of our history?" They are right. Their imputation of evil motives to all other parties, their assumption that no guarantees can be relied on, their fear that even their best friends might betray them—these are all normal responses to the kind of horrors that they and their forebears have gone through. Unless an outsider can understand that outlook and can, taking it into account, pursue the effort to find solutions to the practical problems that the area faces, he or she will not make much of a contribution.

Let me turn now to the other side, the Palestinians and the Egyptians. Between our team and the Palestinians there were certain barriers—some ours, some theirs. There were some personalities with whom we thought it unwise to attempt to cultivate a friendship, and there were some who would not have anything to do with us. I encountered one of those individuals who fell in the latter category on the street one day. He is a very distinguished Palestinian leader. We had met in New York a year or so earlier, and in fact, he had had dinner at our home. Those of you who are familiar with the compelling strength of Arab hospitality will appreciate his dilemma when he saw his American acquaintance. But he stood on principle; he shook my hand warmly and said that under other circumstances his home would have been our home, but—. We parted agreeing that we had not even met. One may feel that his opposition to Camp David was a tragic mistake; but one can only admire his attachment to principle.

We were, however, able to meet many Palestinians: lawyers, professors, doctors, agronomists, teachers, and others. Almost without exception, they, like the Israelis, wanted to tell us their side of the story. But there was an interesting and rather touching difference in tone between them and the Israelis. Everyone knows that the United States is widely considered to be tilting toward Israel in its policies. Yet, most Israelis tend to assume that a U.S. official whom they may encounter is going to be cool if not hostile in his attitude toward Israel. This is a natural consequence of the Jewish experience, and it is not surprising that one often encounters among Israelis a rather vigorous determination to explain to the presumably ignorant American how things really are.

Among Palestinians, an American encounters a quite different tone. They tend to feel that their cause is so just, so consonant with U.S. ideals—their demand for independence is compared with our Declaration of Independence, their demand for self-determination is related to Wilson's Seventeen Points, and the like—that all decent Americans, even a not-very-decent State Department official, will, they think, be sympathetic. It is only U.S. election politics, they believe, that overrides this sympathy and makes the United States behave in a way which is not, from their viewpoint, even-handed.

This attitude still leaves them with plenty to say to us. And the troubles and complaints that come pouring out are serious indeed. They are, after all, a people under military occupation, more than 13 years of it. It can be defended as a rather well-conducted occupation, but it has not been a pleasure cruise. And for understandable reasons, the occupation has become more onerous in the years since Camp David, as both sides have tried to strengthen their positions for the eventual negotiation and settlement.

The Palestinians have prospered in a number of respects during the occupation, but they point out that almost every element of this prosperity has its reverse side. If a man has made money, what is he to do with it? The Arab banks were closed in 1967; he refuses to deposit it in an Israeli bank, and investment is difficult. Many Palestinians have jobs in Israel, but it is generally to do menial work the Israelis no longer want to take on. If his son goes to an Israeli college, he is not likely to find any sort of decent job after graduation. Does he want to start a business in the West Bank? He will probably need a permit from the military government, and there may be long delays, especially if he would be competing with Israeli firms. Would he and some friends want to start an orphanage, a technical school, or a college? He may be told there are already too many of these institutions.

But far more important than these various harassments and constraints is the question of the land. How could our fathers and grandfathers have failed to understand, one Israeli writer has asked, how deeply the Palestinian peasants were attached to the soil? This was, after all, the same land to which the Jews had retained such strong emotional and religious links through all their wanderings. And the Palestinian peasants had been sitting there on it, cultivating it from generation to generation, maybe for many centuries.

Today in the West Bank, the Palestinians fear that they are to be the powerless, helpless witnesses of a process that will eventually transform the Arab character of what is left, the rocky hills that the Israelis call Judea and Samaria, much as the coastal plain has been transformed from Arab to Jewish dominance over the past two generations. The Palestinians see the Israeli program of building settlements as the leading edge of this contemplated transformation. For this reason, there is no other question whose disposition, one way or another, will have nearly as great an impact on the prospects for peace as this profoundly conflicted problem of land.

We have noted the anxieties an Israeli parent must often feel over children who fail to come home on schedule. Palestinian parents are also fearful and anxious, constantly on edge. A tardy child might, for example, have been pulled off a bus at a military checkpoint. It may then have been pushed around, may even have sassed an Israeli soldier and risked being beaten or arrested. The child may have been caught up in a sweep of Arab bystanders if a bomb went off near where it happened to be. Or it may have joined in a student demonstration, shouting slogans or throwing rocks. A number of things including pure chance could have landed the child in a hospital or in detention. Or the child might, in fact, be a Palestine Liberation Organization (PLO) activist, perhaps without the parents being aware of it, and the tardiness may simply be a result of having been caught by Israeli security forces.

The unhappy and sometimes tragic events of this type, events that characterize any military occupation, are, one should note, quite effectively reported and appropriately criticized in the Israeli press, which rarely handles the shortcomings of the Israeli government with kid gloves. Regrettably, like Palestinian terrorism, such events continue to occur, and they continue to discredit those who attempt to justify or excuse them.

We have spoken of Israeli paranoia and of its basis in the facts of life and history. We should now note the prevalence of Palestinian paranoia and its basis in facts and personal experiences. What has a Palestinian man of about 60 seen in his lifetime?

He was born in an area just liberated from centuries of Turkish misrule and oppression. As he grew up, he became aware that he was living in one of the centers of the new Arab nationalism and cultural revival, an area that had been cheated of its independence by the British after they had made conflicting promises in World War I to Arab and Jewish leaders—promises about who was to get what in a land that they, the British, did not own. In his school years he saw the conflict intensifying as a result of the growth of the Jewish minority—or, as one Arab friend has described to me one of his earliest memories, he came home from school to see his home being blown up by the authorities, a punishment for his father's support of Arab agitation against British policies.

As a young man, our typical Palestinian might have served in the British administration, perhaps at the same time sympathizing with Hitler's Germany, which he thought of only as the enemy of his British enemy. He would tend not to believe the stories of Hitler's persecution of the Jews. He might have joined in the irregular warfare against the Jews, which he looked upon as legitimate defense against a foreign invader. Then in 1947 and 1948, when the British gave up their effort to maintain order, he would have witnessed with astonishment the Jewish victory not merely over local Palestinian forces but over the combined Arab armies that attacked the new state of Israel, vowing to push it into the sea. And he would have seen this humiliation repeated twice more, in 1956 and 1967, the last of these Arab defeats bringing the Israeli military occupation of what he as a child thought would someday become his country. Life has seemed to this man and to his children to be an unbroken chain of defeats, betrayals, and humiliations. He is bitter, not just toward Israelis, but toward Arab governments, toward his own ineffective and unwise leaders, and toward Western governments, especially the United States. He had a moment of pride and hope after the 1973 war. It showed that Arabs can fight, and for the first time, a war did not end in a total Israeli victory. But he is again bitter toward Egypt, which disappointed and/or betrayed his hopes through negotiations that seem to him to have sold off Palestinian rights for the sand and oil of the Sinai.

Some—a few—of the Palestinians we knew would admit to mixed feelings about the peace policies started by the slain President Sadat. The Palestinians, like other Arabs, are intensely romantic, and like most romantics they tend to claim they are very hardheaded and pragmatic. From a strictly practical, Egyptian viewpoint, they acknowledge that President Sadat made a good bargain and would support President Mubarak's effort to continue the peace process. Some will even admit that both Egyptian leaders have continued to push hard on the problem of Palestinian rights. This steadfastness has surprised many and impressed a few. But then, these Palestinians are likely to be even more bitter toward the United States, whom they accuse of pressing Sadat at Camp David to accept vague Israeli promises and of then failing to follow through effectively on the political and moral obligations that the United States implicitly had taken on itself.

When contemporary history is seen through the eyes of people whose experiences have been of this character, is it any wonder that paranoia becomes a fair description of their state of mind? The Middle Eastern conflict is often described as a conflict not between right and wrong but between two rights. That is a fair description; but the task of reconciling two conflicting rights is not unusual in diplomacy. In the Middle East, this task is made far more difficult by the fact that each right is defended by a party in the grip of a paranoia—and a thoroughly justified paranoia.

A word about the Egyptians, among whom we also spent many months, is also in order. Two things struck us about Egypt, as they

160 / ISRAEL, THE MIDDLE EAST, & U.S. INTERESTS

have struck many visitors. Among all the Arabs, as is well known, there is a powerful code of personal behavior toward strangers, a code that involves much more than mere forms of courtesy. Except where individual attitudes have been poisoned by politics or poverty, the traveler in the Arab world meets genuine warmth and a sincere welcome. But in Egypt there is something more. People who have traveled widely are constantly trying to put a finger on it, and the best they seem to be able to come up with is to say that the Egyptians are just about the nicest people anywhere, and this is a quality that runs from the top officials to the poorest peasant. "Affability," says a perceptive Israeli traveler of 1980 quoting a British traveler of 150 years earlier, "is a general characteristic of Egyptians of all classes."[1]

The second quality that strikes visitors is Egyptian self-confidence, a sense of being someone: the heir of a great culture, a member of a nation in the Western sense. One Israeli friend spoke of them admiringly, even enviously, as the only people he knew who simply sat down beside a river, back before history began, and stayed there ever since.

Egypt has had a central role in each of the wars against Israel. In fact, it is often said that the Arabs have no real military option against Israel without Egypt. A great many Egyptians died in those wars. One of our drivers in Cairo remarked that in 1967 he was the only man in his battalion who was not killed or wounded when the unit was caught in the open by Israeli aircraft. So the defeats of 1948, 1956, and 1967 were bitter for proud Egyptians, and the losses were cruel. But seen in the long perspective of Egyptian history, these could be considered minor setbacks; Egyptian national existence was hardly in question. The war of 1973 revived Egyptian pride in their fighting qualities and their leaders.

The tone in which Egyptians discuss the Middle Eastern problem is thus very different from that used by Palestinians. Egyptians are not paranoid. Today, they are not so much bitter at Israel as perplexed by what they consider Israeli shortsightedness in failing to take full advantage of the opportunities Sadat had opened to them. Just as they are confident in their own Egyptian destiny, they are confident that the Palestinians will survive as a people and find their Palestinian destiny, confident that someday there will be peace between Israelis and Palestinians, peace on honorable terms, satisfactory to all but the most extreme on either side. But the road to that peace can be long or short, smooth or rough, they argue, and if the present favorable moment is not seized, the next phase could be more costly and more dangerous to all.

One must be quite clear. The Egyptians are not threatening a renewal of fighting or war. That phase is past; the war of 1973, the

October war, was "the last war." The recorded voice of President Sadat had repeated that assurance ten times a day on a private Israeli radio station, the Voice of Peace, as President Mubarak's similar statements are stated and restated constantly by the same medium, and Egyptians at all levels repeat it with what I judge to be total sincerity.

But, the Egyptians continue, real peace between two old enemies cannot be made in a day. The Palestinians are brothers, and if the Israelis refuse to deal seriously and generously with the Palestinian problem, then the leaders who have come after Sadat are likely to be less patient, less accommodating, more harsh if you will, than Sadat had been in the initial period after Camp David.

Let us try now to draw some conclusions from our inconclusive dealings with the Middle Eastern problem, from the priceless opportunity to live for a year and a half in the middle of the problem and in the midst of the people whose lives unavoidably are totally wrapped up in the problem, wholly dominated by its ups and downs. What are the prospects for peace?

First, what is sometimes called the Hundred Years War is not yet over. There is no war at the moment, and there is reason to hope that Sadat's words about "the last war" are not only a sincere promise, but an accurate prophecy. But having reason to hops is not the same as being certain or confident.

Yet, if this Hundred Years War, this struggle over the possession or the partition of the land called Palestine, the land the Israelis call Eretz Yisrael ("the Land of Israel"), is not yet over, it has surely reached the beginning of the end. In spite of the tragic slaying of President Sadat, there still is peace, the beginning of real peace, between Israel and the largest Arab state. And from our experience one can reasonably feel high confidence that the Egyptians will try very hard indeed to make that peace work. One can understand Israeli impatience at the slow pace of development of Israeli-Egyptian bilateral relations. One can understand Israeli misgivings about "after Sadat." But that impatience and those misgivings are not well founded. They do not take proper account of the enormous change that Sadat has brought about.

Second, if one turns from the Israeli-Egyptian relationship to the Israeli-Palestinian relationship that lies so much closer to the heart of the Middle Eastern problem, then it is difficult to be so optimistic, at least with respect to the short term. Throughout this hundred years of struggle, there has always been a bad problem of communication between those Arabs and Jews who were in such close, daily contact. Very few made the effort that should have been made to see the situation from the other side. Witness the famous Zionist slogan A land without people for a people without land; and witness the Arab refusal to acknowledge or understand the ghastly realities that were driving the Jews out of Europe. Today, after so many years of bitter conflict, the chasm across which Israelis and Palestinians are shouting at each other is frighteningly wide. It was a rare privilege for us on the U.S. negotiating team to watch Israelis and Egyptians learning to talk to each other, even learning to trust each other as human beings. But that process has hardly begun between Palestinians and Israelis, even though today they mingle freely and speak each other's languages in a most impressive way.

There are a few on each side who have developed the capacity to see how things look from the other side. But here we encounter one of those asymmetries that plague the Middle Eastern problem and contribute to misunderstandings even among those who are trying very hard to understand. The Israelis trying to bridge the chasm are very articulate. They organize and agitate and publish, and they make a real impression among both Israelis and Arabs, even though they are a relatively small group within Israel.

Such people also exist on the Palestinian side, as our team could testify from long discussions with some of them. But these Palestinian doves fail to come out in the open with their views, or they publish them in such ambiguous and obscure ways that they are without resonance in either Palestinian or Israeli circles.

The sad consequence of these poor and asymmetrical communications is that even when moderates on one or the other side are formulating proposals that they believe could lead out of the present deadlock, the concessions and assurances that they formulate rarely ring any bells on the other side. They simply do not go to the needs and fears of the other party.

A third conclusion from our experiences is more cheerful: it is that the problem can be solved. That may not sound like much of a conclusion—something between a mere truism and a worthless piece of positive thinking from Pangloss. But it is certainly not a mere truism. Given the intensity of the feelings on both sides, the interacting cases of acute paranoia, and some knowledge of how rather similar problems—say, Northern Ireland—have evolved and persisted and grown ever more intractable for centuries, it is really rather bold to assert that a Middle Eastern solution in the reasonably near future is possible. But this assertion is not made without any solid basis, for if the views and attitudes toward possible elements of solutions that we have heard put forward privately by both Israelis and Palestinians can somehow be properly organized and presented to the other side, then a successful negotiation—long, difficult, and probably moving by stages as mutual confidence grows—really can come about.

It was one stage in that long process that was addressed by the negotiation in which we were involved under the leadership first of

Robert Strauss, then of Sol Linowitz. It had been correctly decided at Camp David that the problem had to progress through stages as real communications were developed among the parties and confidence was built. Despite Palestinian and Jordanian rejection of the Camp David framework, it was our hope in early 1979 that reasonable proposals for a next stage, autonomy, could be formulated by the three Camp David partners and could convince the Palestinians that going down our road could take them in the direction they want to go. Obviously, we did not achieve our objectives, certainly not in the time available. Especially now that President Mubarak has taken effective control over the continuity of negotiations, a new team must now consider what the possibilities are. But reviewing our experience during that year and a half, I am convinced more than ever that the elements of the process as they were envisaged at Camp David were basically correct.

Here we come to our final conclusion: an active U.S. role is not merely useful, it is essential. Even to produce a one-sentence communiqué after one of our negotiating sessions, the U.S. team almost always had to get rather heavily into the act. Both parties found it easier (though not easy) to make concessions to the middleman than to each other. Today, the factors hampering communication and eventual negotiation between Palestinians and Israelis are much too powerful to be overcome without outside help. And that outside help can only come from the United States. Our communications with both sides are far from free of tension and misunderstanding, but real communication with both can and does take place. Arabs and Israelis, on the other hand, have for too long communicated primarily with weapons. When they have used words, it has primarily been rhetoric, rhetoric tuned to each side's own internal audience. This is a heavy legacy. It leaves both sides inescapably dependent on some third party. Even after Sadat had taken the extraordinary step of going to Jerusalem, there would not, I think, have been a Camp David framework or an Egyptian-Israeli peace treaty without the enormous efforts put into the task by President Jimmy Carter, Secretary of State Cyrus Vance, and their staffs. The role of the United States in assisting future advances will continue to be crucial.

One of the gravest responsibilities facing President Reagan's administration is how to construct an effective follow-up to the Camp David achievements. He will need our best wishes and our strongest support in that task.

NOTE

1. Amos Elon, <u>Flight into Egypt</u> (New York: Doubleday, 1980), quoting Edward Lane, <u>The Manners and Customs of the Modern Egyptians</u> (London: C. Knight, 1836).

INDEX

Afghanistan, xiii, 97, 101, 103, 126, 128, 130, 131, 132-33, 134, 147
Albania, 93, 131
Algeria, 140
Alroy, David, 9
Angola, 101, 127, 128, 130, 131, 132
Arab nationalism, 21, 27, 29, 31, 91, 92, 143, 145
Arabs, 21-23, 29, 144
Arafat, Yasser, 107, 113
Assad, Hafez, 100, 102, 118-19
Aswan High Dam, 91, 92
autonomy negotiations, 28, 32, 153-63

Ba'thism, 29
Begin, Menachem, xvii, 28-29, 30, 109, 112, 114, 115
Benjamin of Tudela, 10
Bethlehem, 4
Bible, 4
Boulding, Kenneth, 18-19
Brezhnev, Leonid I., 97, 105, 131, 132
Brzezinski, Zbigniew, xiii, 73-74, 132
Bulgaria, 107

Camp David xiv, 26, 27-28, 29, 31-32, 71, 96, 107, 115, 128, 157, 163
Carter, President Jimmy, xvii, 28-29, 32, 67, 75, 128, 163
Ceauşescu, Nicolae, 109-21
Chervonenko, S. R., 131-32
China, People's Republic of, 91, 92, 126, 131, 141, 146

Christianity in the Middle East, 3-14
COMECON, 105-6, 110, 120
Comintern, 134
Czechoslovakia, 107, 131, 141

Dayan, Moshe, 29
Deutsch, Karl, 20

East Germany, 107
Eastern Europe and the Middle East, 105-21
Egypt, 26-28, 29-31, 46-47, 69, 71, 72, 76, 77-78, 82, 85, 91-94, 96, 97, 112-13, 118, 128, 129, 139-40, 153, 159-61
Egyptian-Syrian federation, 93
Eisenhower, President Dwight, xv, 90
Emden, Rabbi Jacob, 11
energy independence, xvi, 84
Epictetus, 18
Ethiopia, 101, 128, 131, 133

Galilee, 4, 10-11
Geiger, Abraham, 13
Gheorghiu-Dej, Gheorghe, 110
Glückel of Hamel, 9-10
Golan Heights, xv, 119
Greece, 135, 136, 137

Haig, Alexander, 32
Ha-Levi, Yehudah, 8, 9
Heikal, Mohammed, 126-27
Hitler, Adolf, 89, 133, 135
hostages, U.S., in Iran, 32
Hungary, 108
Hussein, King, 71

Iran, 45-46, 67, 70, 73-79, 90-91, 92, 97, 99, 101, 115-17, 126-29, 133, 134, 135, 136, 137, 148; and hostage crisis, 32; and war with Iraq, 70, 72, 100, 101, 115, 128
Iraq, 29, 67, 68, 69, 70, 85, 91-92, 94, 97, 99, 107, 112-13, 115, 116, 117, 129, 140
Islam, 3, 4, 9, 31, 141; and Islamic revival, 73-79
Israel, xiii, xv-xvi, 3-14, 20-23, 26-31, 37-49, 51-62, 67, 69, 71, 72, 76, 80-85, 90, 93, 94, 100, 107, 108, 109, 111-12, 114, 115, 120, 128, 141, 142-43, 153, 154-59, 161-62
Israeli agriculture, 37-49, 51-62
Israeli-Egyptian peace treaty, 26-31, 161, 163

Janis, Irving, 20
Jerusalem, 4, 5, 6-7, 10, 12, 13
Jesus of Nazareth, 3
Jordan, 68, 69, 71, 72, 82-83, 112, 113, 118, 119, 163
Judaism, 3-14

Kadar, Janos, 108
Kenya, 71
Khomeini, Ayatollah, 128
Khrushchev, Nikita, 92, 97, 99, 137
Kissinger, Henry, 30, 67, 73, 75, 95
Kuwait, 70, 99, 115-16, 117

Lebanon, 29, 31, 67, 68, 82, 92, 100, 102, 112, 119
Levi, Werner, 20
Libya, 85, 101, 115-17, 129, 136
Linowitz, Sol, 163
Luria, Isaac, 11

Maimonides, 6
Merritt, Richard, 20

Mirskii, G. I., 97
Molotov, V. M., 89, 135, 136
Morocco, 68
Mozambique, 133
Mubarak, President Hossni, 159, 163
Muhammad, 4

Nasser, President Gamal A., 69, 91-93, 94, 99, 100, 108, 127
Nasserism, 29, 83, 99
Nixon, President Richard, 67, 73, 75, 95
North Atlantic Treaty Organization (NATO), 143

oil, 30, 74-76, 84, 105-6, 108, 115-17, 127
Oman, 74
Organization of Petroleum Exporting Countries (OPEC), 30, 74, 75, 106, 108, 114, 116, 118, 121

Pakistan, 132
Palestine, 13, 145, 155
Palestine Liberation Organization (PLO), 32, 67, 102, 107, 109, 111-15
Palestinians, 28, 33, 119, 153, 154, 156-59, 160, 161, 162, 163
pan-Arabism, 22, 31
Peres, Shimon, 112
Persian Gulf, xiii, 31, 67, 69-70, 75, 82, 97, 102, 120, 127, 129; sheikhdoms in, 68, 70
Podgorny, Nikolai, 138
Poland, 108

Qaddafi, Moammar, 99
Qasim, Abd al-Karim, 92, 99

rapid deployment force, xvi, 70
Reagan, President Ronald, xvi, 32, 67, 128, 163
Reform Judaism, 13

religious groups, 3-14, 73-79, 141-42; and nationalism, 141-46

Sadat, President Anwar, xvii, 26, 28, 30, 31, 77, 78, 95-96, 99, 109, 112, 113, 114, 118-19, 127, 128, 159, 161
Sandburg, Carl, xiv
Saudi Arabia, 45, 67, 68-69, 70-71, 76, 78-79, 82, 100, 115, 116
SAVAK, 76
Sharabi, Hisham, 21
Shelepin, Alexander, 138
Shi'ites, 73, 78
Smith, Brewster, 20
Soviet Union, 89-103, 107-8, 126-48; and interests in Middle East, xv, 23, 74, 76, 89-103, 112-13, 126-48; and policies toward nationalism, 142-46
Stalin, 90, 135-36, 137, 141-42, 143, 145
Strauss, Robert, 163
Sudan, 71, 140
Syria, 29, 44-45, 68, 69, 96, 99-100, 107, 112-13, 118, 129, 140

Tito, 108-9
Tudeh (Communist) party, 76, 129
Turkey, 90, 91, 97, 99, 126, 134, 135-36, 143-44, 145, 146

United States: interests in Middle East, xiv-xvi, 67, 69-72, 114, 132, 136, 147; policy toward Iran, 73-79, 80-85

Vance, Cyrus, 163
Vital, Hayyim, 11

Weizman, Ezer, 29
White, Ralph, 20

Yemen, North, 68, 69, 99, 133
Yemen, South, 68, 69, 70, 93, 99, 100, 107, 128
Yom Kippur (Ramadan) War of 1973, 30, 94-95, 101, 109, 112, 138, 160-61
Yugoslavia, 108-9, 111, 131

Zevi, Shabbetai, 9
Zionism, 7-14, 22, 161

ABOUT THE EDITORS AND CONTRIBUTORS

HARRY S. ALLEN is the Director of Institutional Research and Planning at the University of Nebraska-Lincoln. He received his Master of Science degree from the University of Denver and specializes in Middle Eastern affairs.

IVAN VOLGYES is Professor of Political Science and Director of Slavic and East European Studies at the University of Nebraska-Lincoln. He is the author or editor of more than 20 books and several scores of articles dealing with Eastern Europe and the USSR. His latest book, The Political Reliability of the Warsaw Pact, was published by Duke University Press in 1982.

EDMUND S. MUSKIE was the 58th U.S. Secretary of State. He graduated cum laude from Bates College in Lewiston, Maine, in 1936, where he was a Phi Beta Kappa. In 1939 he received his law degree from Cornell University Law School. Mr. Muskie was elected to the Maine House of Representatives in 1946, 1948, and 1950. He was elected Governor of Maine in 1954 and served two terms before being elected to the U.S. Senate in 1958. During his 22 years in the Senate, he served on the Foreign Relations Committee, the Governmental Affairs Committee, the Environment and Public Works Committee, and as Chairman of the Senate Committee on the Budget. He has traveled extensively throughout Europe, the Middle East, and Asia.

VERNON V. ASPATURIAN is Evan Pugh Professor of Political Science and Director of the Slavic and Soviet Language and Area Center at Pennsylvania State University. He received his Ph.D. from the University of California-Los Angeles and has been a Distinguished Visiting Professor at UCLA, Columbia University, the School of Advanced International Studies-Johns Hopkins University, the Naval Postgraduate School, and at the Graduate Institute of International Affairs, Geneva, Switzerland. He has also been a consultant to the Rand Corporation, the U.S. Office of Education, the Army War College, and at the Center for Strategic Studies. He is the author and editor of 6 books and 60 articles, and has served as an expert witness to the U.S. Congress.

TODD ENDELMAN received his Ph.D. from Harvard University and is a Professor of History and Jewish Studies at Indiana University. He has also taught at Harvard University, Yeshiva University, and Hebrew Union College. He is the author of a book and several articles dealing with the problems of Judaism. He has also received the Gerrard and Ella Berman National Jewish Book Award for the best work on Jewish history published in 1979 for The Jews of Georgian England. This book also was awarded the A. S. Diamond Memorial Prize. He is also the recipient of a National Endowment for the Humanities Fellowship and is a member of the Board of Editors of the AJS Review.

TROND GILBERG received his Ph.D. from the University of Wisconsin. He is currently a Professor of Political Science and Associate Director of the Soviet and Slavic Language and Area Center at Pennsylvania State University and Visiting Professor of Political Science at the U.S. Military Academy at West Point. In addition to grants from the American Council of Learned Societies and the International Research and Exchanges Board to do fieldwork in Romania, he has also served as a Visiting Professor at Christian-Albrechts University and at the University of Washington. He is the author of 2 books on international politics and has contributed 20 articles and chapters to scholarly volumes.

C. DON GUSTAFSON received his M.S. from Colorado State University and has done postmaster's study at Colorado State University, the University of Arkansas, the University of California, and at San Diego State. He is currently Farm Adviser for the Cooperative Agricultural Extension of the University of California-San Diego County. He has written more than 100 articles for trade journals, scientific journals, and scientific meetings. He is a consultant on avocados, citrus, and irrigation technology to many countries, including Israel, South America, Mexico, South Africa, and Cameroon.

MICHAEL HANDEL received his Ph.D. from Harvard University, where he has been a Research Associate for the Harvard University Center for International Affairs since 1979. He has been Professor of International Affairs at the Israeli War College, the Hebrew University, and at the University of Massachusetts. He is the author of five books and many articles. His last volume, Surprise in Diplomacy: Hitler, Stalin, Sadat, was published in 1981 by the Harvard University Center for International Affairs.

NICKI KEDDIE received her Ph.D. from the University of California at Berkeley. She is a Professor of History at the University of California at Los Angeles. She has held most of the major prestigious fellowships offered in the fields of the social sciences and humanities, including those granted by the Rockefeller, Guggenheim, and Ford foundations. She has published seven books on the Middle East, including Women in the Muslim World and The Middle East and Beyond. In addition to her books, she has also written more than 70 articles and chapters for scholarly volumes dealing with the Middle East in general, and with Iran in particular.

JAMES LEONARD, a Princeton graduate, has been a foreign service officer since 1948. He served as the U.S. Representative and Assistant Director of the Geneva Disarmament Committee and as the U.S. Deputy Special Negotiator—first under Robert Strauss, then under Sol Linowitz—in the autonomy negotiations called for under the Camp David Agreement. From May 1979 to January 1981 he resided in the area, shuttling between Egypt and Israel as the three negotiating teams wrestled with the problem of autonomy for the West Bank and Gaza.

CYRUS McKELL received his Ph.D. from Oregon State University. He has been Director of the Institute for Land Rehabilitation at Utah State University since 1976. He is a Professor of Range Sciences at Utah State University. He is author of 149 articles and has done major research directed toward land resources ecology and physiology of rangeland plants. His publications also include the coauthoring of two books entitled Biology and Utilization of Grasses and Useful Wildland Shrubs.

AMOS PERLMUTTER received his Ph.D. from the University of California at Berkeley and is a Professor of Political Science and Sociology at the American University in Washington, D.C. In addition to his current position, he has been Ford Professor of Political Science at MIT and has been a Fellow at the Woodrow Wilson International Center for Scholars, the Center for International Affairs at Harvard, and the Brookings Institution. He has written 9 books and 35 articles in scholarly journals, as well as frequent columns for the Wall Street Journal, the Los Angeles Times, the Long Island Newsday, the New York Times, the New Republic, Harper's, Reader's Digest, Commentary, Newsweek, and U.S. News and World Report. He is also the editor of the Journal of Strategic Studies. His new volume, entitled International Politics and Crisis Management: Middle East 1967-1979, was published in 1981.

ALVIN Z. RUBINSTEIN received his Ph.D. from, and is Professor of Political Science at, the University of Pennsylvania. He has also been a Distinguished Visiting Professor at many institutions and an Associate of the Russian Research Center at Harvard University. In addition to a large number of articles, he is also the author of 11 books, including Soviet Foreign Policy since World War II: Imperial and Global and Red Star on the Nile: The Soviet-Egyptian Influence Relationship since the June War. He is a member of the editorial boards of Orbis, Soviet Union, Current History, and Studies in Comparative Communism.

ABDUL AZIZ SAID, Professor of International Studies in the School of International Service of the American University, is one of the foremost specialists on international politics and foreign policy. In addition to several dozens of articles in scholarly journals, he is the author of 11 books on foreign policy. His most recent volume is entitled Human Rights and World Order. He is the Associate Editor of Society Magazine, a consultant to the Department of State, and a frequent lecturer at the service academies of the United States.

HAIM SHAKED received his Ph.D. from the University of London, School for Oriental and African Studies. He is Professor of Middle Eastern History, Shiloah Center for Middle Eastern History, Tel Aviv University, Tel Aviv, Israel. He is author of The Life of the Sudanese Mahdi and the editor of a number of books on the Middle East, including From June to October: The Middle East between 1970-73, The Middle East and the United States, and the Middle East Contemporary Survey, of which three volumes have already appeared. He also received a distinguished British Council Fellowship. He is currently on sabbatical leave as Visiting Professor with the Departments of Political Science and History, York University, Downsview, Ontario, Canada.

ALAIN SPORTICHE is a Graduate Fellow at the School of International Studies at the American University in Washington, D.C., where he specializes in Middle Eastern studies.